ENVIRONMENTAL HUMANITIES: A RETHINKING OF LANDSCAPE ARCHAEOLOGY?

ENVIRONMENTAL HUMANITIES: A RETHINKING OF LANDSCAPE ARCHAEOLOGY?

INTERDISCIPLINARY ACADEMIC RESEARCH RELATED TO DIFFERENT PERSPECTIVES OF LANDSCAPES

editors
Sjoerd Kluiving, Kerstin Liden
& Christina Fredengren

© 2021 Individual authors

Published by Sidestone Press, Leiden
www.sidestone.com

Imprint: Sidestone Press Academics

Lay-out & cover design: Sidestone Press
Photograph cover: painting by George Hendrik Breitner (A Heath Landscape, Presumably in Drenthe, The Netherlands; c. 1880 - c. 1923; coll. Rijksmuseum Amsterdam SK-A-3533)

ISBN 978-94-6427-003-7 (softcover)
ISBN 978-94-6427-004-4 (hardcover)
ISBN 978-94-6427-005-1 (PDF e-book)

Contents

Environmental humanities a rethinking of landscape archaeology? Sjoerd Kluiving, Kerstin Lidén & Christina Fredengren	7
Nature and society: an integrated multi-perspective landscape approach in practice Oscar Jacobsson	13
Travel books as landscape archaeology reports Francoise Besson	31
Fragments of the Wild: Wordsworth's Yew Trees and Contemporary Archaeology Andrew Hoaen	47
Geological and historical findings reveal differential anthropogenic substrate control in unique streets of Diemen, The Netherlands Ronald van Gelder, Sjoerd Kluiving, Inger Leemans, Ruben den Ouden & Jan Goedhart	69
Re-thinking Deep Time Landscapes Christina Fredengren	91
Published books in the CLUES series	107

Environmental humanities a rethinking of landscape archaeology?

Sjoerd Kluiving [a], Kerstin Lidén[b] &
Christina Fredengren[b]

a. Vrije Universiteit Amsterdam, Faculty of Humanities/CLUE+/Environmental Humanities Center, The Netherlands
b. Stockholm University, Department of Archaeology and Classical Studies, Sweden

Landscape archaeology has often focused on how the environment has been experienced and meaningfully captured by the human agent, thereby having a rather anthropocentric focus. However, with the material turn in archaeology and the emerging approaches within the Environmental Humanities (see Rose et. al 2012), as well as the interdisciplinary nature of landscape archaeology at LAC meetings (see Kluiving & Guttmann, 2012) – new forms of research have started to appear. In this special issue we present a set of papers with a tradition of interdisciplinary research in geology and archaeology related to different perspectives of landscapes. A major question in this publication is how can the landscape concept be revitalised and changed by taking a critical look at nature/culture relationships and benefit from moving beyond a social constructivist backing for landscape theory?

There has been an increasing archaeological interest in human-animal-nature relations, where archaeology has shifted from a focus on deciphering meaning, or understanding symbols and the social construction of the landscape to an acknowledgement of how things, places and the environment contribute with their own agencies to the shaping of relations. This means that the environment cannot be regarded as a blank space that landscape meaning is projected onto. Parallel to this, the field of environmental humanities poses the question of how to work with the intermeshing of humans and their surroundings. To allow the environment back in as an active agent of change, means that landscape archaeology can deal better with issues such as global warming, an escalating loss of biodiversity as well as increasingly toxic environment. However, this does not leave human agency out of the equation. It is humans who reinforce the environmental challenges of today. The scholarly field of the humanities deal with questions like how is meaning attributed, what cultural factors drive human action, what role is played by ethics, how is landscape experienced emotionally, as well as how concepts derived from art, literature, and history function in such processes of meaning attribution and other cultural processes. This humanities approach is of utmost importance when dealing with climate and environmental challenges ahead and we need a new landscape archaeology that meets these challenges, but also that meets well across disciplinary boundaries. Here inspiration can be found in discussions with scholars in the emerging field of Environmental Humanities.

Originally the abrupt change of the Industrial Revolution at the end of the eighteenth century was regarded as the starting point of the Anthropocene – the Age of Humans- (Crutzen & Stoermer 2000), although a majority of the Anthropocene Working Group appears to vote for a start date of the Anthropocene at AD 1950.[1] The start of the Anthropocene still remains somewhat open and is a contentious term, but the discussions by scholars about the wisdom of adopting it have been eclipsed by its popularity in public debate. Basically the idea is that humans have started changing the earth to the extent that humanity has become a geological force. The most important question in the Anthropocene discussion comes down to the following: how are we going to deal with the desired energy-, water, food- nexus and other transitions in order to preserve our planet? Many scholarly disciplines contribute to this contemporary discussion. At some universities, disciplines traditionally called 'humanities', group themselves in a cluster called 'Environmental Humanities,' including environmental history, eco-criticism (literature studies), eco-art studies etc.[2] The special role of historians in this group is offering practices tested in the laboratory of the past, in addition to for instance art projects and literary images of the present, or artistic and literary fantasies about the future. This interdisciplinary collaboration contributes to increasing awareness of and identification with the highly desired transition and preservation of the earth (Ritson 2019).

In an effort to capture the environmental humanities DB Rose et al. have formulated the following: "The humanities have traditionally worked with questions of meaning, value, ethics, justice and the politics of knowledge production. In bringing these questions into environmental domains, we are able to articulate a 'thicker' notion of humanity, one that rejects reductionist accounts of self-contained, rational, decision making subjects. Rather, the environmental humanities positions us as participants in lively ecologies of meaning and value, entangled within rich patterns of cultural and historical diversity that shape who we are and the ways in which we are able to 'become with' others" (Rose et al 2012, 1).

While this framing is just one of many interpretations, it invigorates current interdisciplinary research on the environment, in response to a growing interest around the world in the many questions that arise in this era of rapid climatic, environmental and social change. The Environmental Humanities is an emerging interdisciplinary area of international research and teaching that addresses contemporary environmental challenges in a way that is historically, philosophically and culturally informed. Environmental Humanities explores questions such as:

---

[1] https://www.theatlantic.com/science/archive/2019/04/great-debate-over-when-anthropocene-started/587194/.

[2] Currently e.g. in Europe: Norway: https://www.ntnu.edu/ikm/environmental-humanities, The Netherlands: www.environmentalhumanitiescenter.com ,Germany: https://www.carsoncenter.uni-muenchen.de/about_rcc/index.html and Ireland: https://www.tcd.ie/tceh/.

What are the historical relations between humans and landscapes? How do fiction and film shape our thinking about climate change? How did people react to floods in the past? How do we compare different time scales in different disciplines?

These questions and many more are at the heart of the Environmental Humanities as well as Landscape Archaeology (cf. Kluiving & Guttmann, 2012, Bebermeier et al, 2012, 2013; Burgers et al, 2016). So as to take stock of the ways in which we interpret the term Environmental Humanities as a rethinking of Landscape Archaeology, we need to ask: Is the broad interdisciplinary arena of Environmental Humanities an acceleration of the process of integration that is central in Landscape Archaeology? Can we envision that future developments, such as the discussion of the Anthropocene concept, are in fact demanding more interdisciplinary collaborations such as Environmental Humanities and Landscape Archaeology?

In this issue Oscar Jacobsson approaches a cross-conceptual perspective in the study of agrarian historical landscapes in Sweden and concludes that future landscape archaeological research has 'a perspective involving a wide theoretical and problematizing approach'. He demonstrates for example that the theme of flooding can be connected to all three perspectives of landscape: the physical, institutional and the symbolic/ideological perspective. He argues that the relationship between human society and the hydrological dynamics of the physical environment has been shaped by multiple levels of agency. How does human-environmental interaction shape symbolical or scenic values? How are institutional factors such as ownership influenced by climatic variations? To what extent are physical landscape changes driven by human symbolical or ideological ideas? These broad and challenging research questions define a rethinking of landscape archaeology that goes beyond the individual 'traditional' disciplines such as archaeology, geology and landscape studies in general.

A relationship with landscapes and with the non-human world is unfolded when the travel book revitalizes the landscape concept. This change in view of the landscape is explored by Francoise Besson. Here travel literature is analysed, *e.g.* how the apparently autobiographical text at times becomes an archaeological report. The intermingling of natural features and human constructions reveals historical layers in the landscape, leading the viewer into ecological awareness. Travel books do not only account for cities, villages, or natural places in the writer's perspective of time and place but also provide them with a sense of observation of the world suggesting a link between all elements.

Just as the landscape bears traces of agriculture, history and religion, it also indicates the temporal changes in the area, as they are signalled by the presence of bridges, in engravings and photographs. Besson also discusses that travel books as archaeological reports are leading to a sense of responsibility and ecological awareness. Travel books look for traces of the past in various geographical areas and so doing they suggest a new way of conceiving our relationship with landscapes.

In an intellectually stimulating review of British history of the wild and the nature, Andrew Hoaen confronts archaeology with observations such as 'beyond the bound'. Regarding landscapes as a static backdrop against ecology, environment and ecological landscape, he also discusses ecocriticism. Taking a contemporary archaeological perspective to environmental problems, Hoaen opens up the possibility for a new understanding of how environments and ecologies come into being and are sustained.

Archaeologists have the methodological tools and long term perspectives that allow us to approach larger issues in the sciences and humanities, and the contemporary world is an excellent laboratory in which to study them.

Western Dutch soil and the subsurface are used to address the development of a 20th century village in the outskirts of Amsterdam, the Netherlands, by Van Gelder et al. This soil is particular suitable to address their research questions because the soil under the roads – built on sunken piles – is easily accessible. Their objectives are to retrieve the geological layers in the soil of a 20th-century neighbourhood, to determine the stratigraphy, as well as the timing of events relating to the time of the 'De Nieuwe Buurt'. In other words, What is the stratigraphical record of the shallow subsurface of Diemen? Do the contemporary layers differ from the layers of the time when the neighbourhood was built? And: can different layers be distinguished within the anthropogenic soil layers in the separately investigated periods?

The western Dutch soft soil seems eminently suitable for research questions related to soil characteristics concerning the so-called 'Anthropocene' debate. This is also the case for the region of Diemen, where the inhabitants already at an early stage had to resort to the raising of the subsiding natural soil with organic and/or inorganic materials. Geological results combined with historical data in the research area reveal impacts of anthropogenic substrate control recorded below the streets of Diemen, resulting in differential settling histories.

The paper by Christina Fredengren brings landscape studies, much used in archaeology and heritage practice, into conversation with the environmental humanities and particularly post-humanist feminist theories. There are connecting points, but also wide differences, where the two major points lie in the centring or decentring of the human, or in how materiality, time and temporality are approached. Introducing some of the major thinkers in this field, the paper deals with how landscapes can be approached as multi-temporal, but present, with spaces for conviviality, but also places where to mourn losses, wounds and sacrifices, as well as to learn how recuperate, practice hospitality and to inherit well. Thereby it starts a discussion on inter- and intra-generational care in heritage policy and practice.

A landscape approach is proposed in conversation with the scholarship that is emerging in the environmental humanities and feminist post-humanism. While both landscape heritage studies and these scholars have the focus on tracing out situated social injustices, the differences lie in the focus on the human and how the factor of time is treated. In heritage studies, the focus is often in the present, while scholarship in the environmental humanities is increasingly interested in both deep time pasts and long-term effects into the future. Furthermore, heritage studies of the social constructivist type often place human perception and experience in the centre. Here post-humanists have started to explore ways of dealing with a world that does not place human well-being as the ethical centre, but instead explore what it would be like if life-cycles, paces and temporalities of a range of more-than-human others as well as materiality were observed. This would have implications for how to approach issues of inter- and intra-generational justice and care, as it would point towards relations of interdependencies between material and multi-species generations.

We propose this set of peer reviewed papers to present new research, where the interdisciplinary Environmental Humanities research meet landscape approaches. There are certainly elements that reflect the process of integration that is central in Landscape Archaeology, such as Hoaen discussing the contemporary archaeological perspective as an approach to environmental problems and how sustainable environments including ecologies can be understood. It is shown by van Gelder et al that the discussion of the Anthropocene concept is demanding increased collaboration between scientific domains, contributing to a much wider interdisciplinary debate that is held nowadays (*e.g.* Burtynski, 2018; Warde et al 2018; Waters et al, 2016). It is stimulating in this issue that the landscape concept is re-vitalised by taking a critical look at nature/culture relationships as discussed by Jacobsson and Besson, and that it benefits from moving beyond a social constructivist backing for landscape theory as discussed by Fredengren. Beyond these it is striking that most papers connect the Environmental Humanities to the Landscape Archaeology with perspectives and questions that relate to sustainability. The next question is to connect the environmental humanist approach to future landscape management in the Anthropocene, which would fit its broad character displayed in this issue, and which will be further explored in future projects.[3]

Acknowledgments

The papers discussed in this special issue originate from the session 'Environmental humanities a rethinking of landscape archaeology?' held at the 4th international Landscape Archaeology Conference (LAC2016), 23rd – 25th August 2016 in Uppsala, Sweden. Editorial reviews of CLUES and EHC greatly improved the quality of this paper. This special issue also benefitted greatly by reviews of Guillermo S. Reher and one anonymous reviewer.

References

Bebermeier, W., Hoelzmann, P., Kaiser, E., & Krause, J. 2013. LAC 2012: 2nd International Landscape and Archaeology Conference, Berlin; Quaternary International, 312, 1-140.

Bebermeier, W., Hebenstreit, R., Kaiser, E., & Krause, J. 2012. Landscape Archaeology Conference (LAC 2012); eTopoi. Journal for Ancient Studies, Special Volume 3, 1-410.

Besson, F. Travel Books as Landscape Archaeology Reports, this issue.

Burgers, G.L.M., Kluiving, S.J., & Hermans, R.A.E. 2016. Multi-, Inter- and Transdisciplinary Research in Landscape Archaeology: Proceedings of the 3rd International Landscape Archaeology Conference in Rome, Italy. University Library, Vrije Universiteit Amsterdam.

Burtynski, E. 2018. Anthropocene. Publisher: Steidl, 236 pages, ISBN-13: 978-3-95829-489-9.

Crutzen, P.J. and Stoermer, E.F. 2000. The "Anthropocene". Global Change Newsletter, 41, 17.

---

3   EU Horizon2020 projects, e.g. www.terranova-itn.eu, https://www.heriland.eu/.

Fredengren, C. Re-thinking Deep Time Landscapes, this issue.

Gelder, R. van, Kluiving, S.J., Leemans, I., Ouden, R. den & Goedhart, J. Geological findings in unique streets of Diemen, The Netherlands, reveal different anthropogenic substrate controlcomplete, this issue.

Hoaen, A. Engaging the senses in the wilder world: Archaeology of the Wild, this issue.

Jacobsson, O. Nature and society: an integrated multi-perspective landscape approach in practice, this issue.

Kluiving, S.J. & Guttmann, E.G.B (eds.) 2012. Landscape Archaeology between Art and Science. From a Multi- to an Interdisciplinary Approach, Landscape & Heritage Studies, Amsterdam University Press, 525 pp. Available in Open Access: http://oapen.org/search?keyword=9789089644183.

Ritson, K. 2019. The shifting sands of the North Sea Low Lands. Routledge Environmental Humanities series. Routledge, New York, 170 p. ISBN 978-1-138-59110-3.

Rose, D.B., Dooren, T. van, Chrulew, M., Cooke, S., Kearnes, M. & O'Gormand, E. 2012. Thinking Through the Environment, Unsettling the Humanities. Environmental Humanities 1 (2012) 1-5, ISSN: 2201-1919.

Warde, P., Robin L. & Sörlin, S. 2018. The Environment- A History of the Idea. JHUP Books, 256 pages. ISBN: 9781421426792.

Waters, C.N., Zalasiewicz, J. Summerhayes C. et al. 2016. "The Anthropocene Is Functionally and Stratigraphically Distinct from the Holocene." Science 351 (6269). DOI:10.1126/science.aad262.

Nature and society: an integrated multi-perspective landscape approach in practice

Oscar Jacobsson[a]

a. Department of Human Geography, Stockholm University, Sweden

Introduction

Agrarian historical landscapes in Sweden have been studied in a great variety of ways. The major works in this field concerning the medieval or Early Modern period have been carried out by historical geographers analysing historical cadastral maps and records using a retrogressive methodology, but contributions have also been made by archaeologists, historians and geologists among others.[1] While previous research has shown the great diversity of historical agrarian practice in Sweden, there has been a tendency to emphasise an empirical approach instead of a wider theoretical-philosophical approach. The empirical practice of agrarian historical landscape research is thus well developed while – simultaneously – there is a lack of theoretical debate.

Watercourses serve as an example of the problems involved in an overly empirical approach. The historical role of watercourses in agrarian landscapes remains rather unknown in Sweden, where streams and rivers have mostly been seen as static objects of human action.[2] This is not only due to limited inter-disciplinary communication, but also to a wider hegemonic role of human-centric landscape perspectives in historical disciplines which only lately has been questioned.[3] Until recently cultural heritage values tied to watercourses remained relatively uncharted territory, despite a long antiquarian tradition of archaeological field surveys in

---

1   Some recent contributions include Olof Karsvall, *Utjordar och Ödegårdar. En studie i retrogressiv metod* (PhD diss., Swedish University of Agricultural Sciences, 2016); Alf Ericsson, *Terra Mediaevalis: jordvärderingssystem i medeltidens Sverige* (PhD diss., Swedish University of Agricultural Sciences, 2012); Per Lagerås , ed. *Environment, Society and the Black Death. An interdisciplinary approach to the Late-Medieval crisis in Sweden* (Oxford: Oxbow Books, 2016).
2   Examples of such an approach include Mona Lorentzon, ed. *Kring Göta Älv – studier i en dalgång* (Gothenburg: Tre Böcker, 1993); Anna Lihammer, 'Landskapet och makten. Området kring Ätran under yngre järnålder och tidig medeltid', in Medeltid i Ätradalen – en resa i fyra etapper, ed Påvel Nicklasson (Stockholm: Almqvist & Wiksell International, 2005): 11-28.
3   E.g. Christina Fredengren', NATURE:CULTURES. Heritage, Sustainability and Feminist Posthumanism' *Current Swedish Archaeology*, 23 (2015): 109-30.

Sweden.⁴ To a certain extent the role of flooding in historical hay-making has been acknowledged in agrarian history and historical geography,⁵ however the focus has been on human-centred factors such as arable fields, ownership patterns and settlement structure. Thus we lack an analysis of human-water relations. In order to develop a holistic view of historical landscape development in Sweden it is vital that integral parts of the analysis are not ignored. Knowledge of the agrarian functions of watercourses cannot be produced by simply gazing at a source material through a traditional lens. Instead other sources and also expanded theoretical perspectives are needed to enable an analysis beyond the anthropocentric and deterministic confines of more classical approaches. Through this, historical landscape research in Sweden could be more fully integrated in the contemporary debate regarding for example climate change and sustainable development.

There is a long tradition of human-environment research in landscape related disciplines, but it is only lately that the interaction between humanity and the physical environment has been analysed as something complex, entwined in a deep two-way communication.⁶ This has led to the development of a wide range of theoretical perspectives, and has also contributed to a wider and integrated discussion in landscape planning.⁷ In more empirical research a similar development can be seen, where a large number of studies have investigated how environment and human activity interact with landscape change.⁸ However, the theoretical discussion is rarely connected to deep empiricism, and empirical research does not often feed-back into a theoretical debate.⁹ Furthermore, theoretically informed empirical landscape research is often confined within disciplinary and geographical boundaries.¹⁰

---

4   Jan Magnusson and Coco Dedering, *VaKul. Vattenförvaltning och kulturmiljö.Slutrapport – etapp 1. Sammanställning av befintligt kunskapsmaterial* (Digital report: Västerhavets vattendistrikt, 2011).
5   E.g. John Granlund, 'Högsby socken och dess byar, näringsliv samt sed och tro'. In *Högsbyboken: Högsby, Långemåla och Fågelfors bygd och liv*, eds Herberth Eriksson and Olle Franzén (Högsby: Högsby kommun, 1969); Coco Dedering, *Kulturhistoria ur dimma: Emåns avrinningsområde* (Kalmar: Länsstyrelsen i Kalmar län, 2001).
6   E.g. Marc Tadaki, Jennifer Salmond, Richard Le Heron and Gary Brierley, 'Nature, culture and the work of physical geography' *Transactions of the institute of British geographers*, 37 (2012): 547-62; Carol P. Harden, 'Framing and Reframing Questions of Human-Environment Interactions', *Annals of the Association of American Geographers*, 102-4 (2012): 737-47; Fredengren,'NATURE:CULTURES'.
7   E.g. Marie Stenseke, 'Integrated landscape management and the complicating issue of temporality', *Landscape Research*, 42-2 (2016): 199-211.
8   E.g. Luigi Bruno, Alessandro Amorosi, Renata Curina, Paolo Severi and Remo Bitelli, 'Human-landscape interactions in the Bologna area (northern Italy) during the mid-late Holocene, with focus on the Roman period' *The Holocene*, 23-11(2013): 1560-1571; Mark G. Macklin, Anna F. Jones and John Lewis, 'River response to rapid Holocene environmental change: evidence and explanation in British catchments' *Quaternary Science Reviews*, 29 (2010): 1555-1576. See also the 2017 issue of Catena on geoarchaeology: Sjoerd Kluiving, Wiebke Bebermeier, Andy Howard and Vanessa M.A. Heyvaert, eds. 'Special section on Geoarchaeology: Human-environment interactions in the Holocene', 149-1(2017): 1-514.
9   For example there are few practical connections between the complex results of geoarchaeology and the theoretical debate concerning culture/nature. Both fit within the wider discussion of the Anthropocene but are seldom allowed to affect each other in practice.
10 A brilliant exception is an article by Katarina Saltzman where she actively engages with a single landscape from several disciplinary perspectives: Katarina Saltzman, 'En stilla och enfallig landsbygd. Konsten att beskriva ett vanligt landskap', in *Moderna landskap. Identifikation och tradition i vardagen*, eds Katarina Saltzman and Birgitta Svensson (Stockholm: Natur och Kultur, 1997): 157-79.

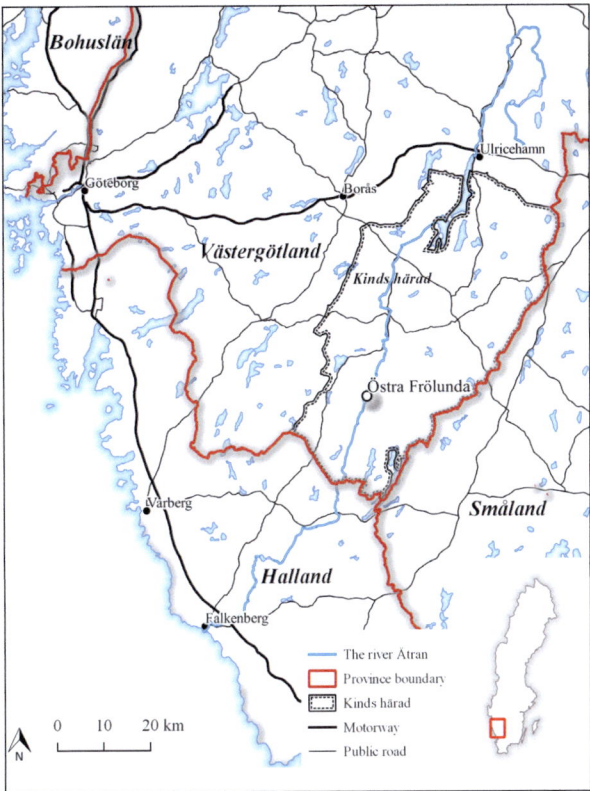

Figure 1. The location of the case study area in south-western Sweden, along with the course of the river Ätran, mentioned administrative boundaries and main present roads. ©Lantmäteriet.

On a certain level the main problem opposing effective communication between different disciplines, approaches and schools of thought is the broad concept of landscape that has been widely and extensively discussed in human geography, physical geography, architecture, history and archaeology. Not only is the concept used differently in each discipline, the perspective used also varies largely according to cultural geographical spaces. Landscape as a theoretical concept is thus used different in Sweden, Italy, England or China. Although the perceptual division becomes clear simply by attending an international conference on landscape research, it is seldom holistically discussed in practice. The different concepts become lenses through which human-environment relations are studied whereas an understanding of the ways in which disparate definitions of landscape connect would contribute to the development of more holistic perspectives.

This paper argues that in order to understand historical processes at work in the Swedish agrarian landscape, it is necessary to use a conceptual framework that recognises the diversity of human relations with the physical environment. This will be done through a case study from Östra Frölunda in south-western Sweden (see Figure 1) focusing mainly on the period between 500-1800 AD. The analysis deals, to a certain extent, with the lack of knowledge concerning riverine landscapes by incorporating physical geographical data and relating this to traditional source material such as historical maps and archaeological sites. A retrogressive historical geographical analysis is used where the results are connected to a broader theoretical scope in order to tackle issues concerning theoretical versus empirical approaches. The problem of conceptual divides in landscape research is discussed in detail and a multi-conceptual framework applied which illuminates the complexity of diverse landscape processes in the studied area. The empirical results presented are developed from a project conducted in 2016 analysing the interaction of floodplains and historical land use in southern Sweden.[11]

Different approaches to landscape

As described above, the study of landscape is complicated in that the word 'landscape' itself can be defined in a variety of ways. A natural starting point of many studies in general landscape history is therefore the *definition* of landscape. For the purposes of this paper it is necessary to give a brief outline of the debate as well as an introduction to the use of this concept in various regions and disciplines, although the subject has been debated almost to exhaustion.

In his article '*Recovering the Substantive Nature of Landscape*' Kenneth Olwig uncovers the history and origin of the landscape concept. The word itself originates from an ancient Germanic concept with a distinctly territorial and communal meaning. This concept can later be found in landscape paintings of the region during the 16th century at a time of a Northern European formation of cultural identity. When imported to the English language from Northern Europe, landscape instead became a scenic concept, mostly due to its blending with national court politics and southern European landscape art, based in ancient Roman and Greek ideals.[12]

In more recent times, landscape as a research concept has been used in a diverse number of ways. Mats Widgren[13] divides landscape into three different concepts which are in use today: landscape as scenery, landscape as institution and land as resource. These concepts are explained below. It should be noted that this division is a rough generalisation of real research practice, where concepts are sometimes blended and used rather differently. As shall be seen however, the generalisation aids in the understanding of a wider pattern of western landscape studies.

The first landscape concept (scenery) is tied to the Anglophone definition described by Olwig, where landscape is a 'way of seeing', exploring representations and mental ideas in a way clearly tied to phenomenology.[14] In a British context, landscape as scenery is commonly found both in geography and archaeology, but in a Scandinavian context this approach is more exclusively tied to landscape archaeological work.[15] The scenic approach to landscape can also be connected to what Alan Baker has termed the post-modern school and while post-modern phenomenology is still very much

---

11 Oscar Jacobsson, Översvämningens landskap: klimatanpassning av åker och äng i det äldre jordbrukslandskapet (Fjällbacka: Kulturlandskapet, 2016).
12 Kenneth R. Olwig,, 'Recovering the Substantive Nature of Landscape', *Annals of the Association of American Geographers* 86-4 (1996): 630-653.
13 Mats Widgren, 'Can landscapes be read?', in *European rural landscapes: persistence and change in a globalising environment*, ed Hannes Palang et al (Boston: Kluwer Academic Publishers, 2004): 455-65.
14 Widgren, 'Can landscapes be read?', 459.
15 For a geographical example, see Veronica della Dora, 'Light and sight: Vesilij Grigorovich Barskij, Mount Athos and the geographies of eighteenth-century Russian Orthodox Enlightenment', *Journal of Historical Geography* 53 (2016):86-103. For a review of phenomenology in archaeology, see Matthew H. Johnson, 'Phenomenological Approaches in Landscape Archaeology', *Annual Review of Anthropology* 41 (2012):269-84.

in use today, theoretical work in geography has developed new forms of this concept building for recent years on post-human research.[16]

The second concept (institution) is instead more directly tied to the Nordic/Germanic meanings of landscape (see above), in which the researcher often explores questions concerning for example power relations, land ownership, organisation and administration. In Sweden this approach is commonly found in historical geography and agrarian history, where questions asked are often tied to the character of the source material. The sources contain a lot of information of a bureaucratic nature concerning land ownership and yearly economic revenues, which becomes important not the least in retrogressive studies.[17]

The third concept (resource) relates to landscape as physical space, which includes land as resource as well as the development of the physical landscape from a combined natural and cultural point-of-view.[18] This concept has been used by both historical and physical geographers in Sweden,[19] and resembles the way in which the term has been used among certain ecologists. For example, Richard Forman and Michel Godron argue that a landscape is a space in which different ecosystems interact in a pattern repeating itself over a larger, not seldom kilometre-wide, area.[20] A landscape in this sense is something measurable and clearly defined, although the use of the term is distinctly unrelated to the etymology of the word itself.

On a general level, most landscape related historical research investigates the ways in which our physical surroundings relate to human society. The 'physical' and 'human' factors involved in the interpretation however vary according to the chosen perspective. A scenic use of landscape is subject-centred and anthropocentric, in that the physical landscape – or nature – only plays an active role through humans. The human agent is often a contemplating one, while the every-day perception resulting from practical engagement with the landscape remains largely ignored.[21] The institutional approach de-individualises the landscape in favour of larger societal structures, ignoring the fact that individuals and subjects constitute the foundation of such structures. Furthermore, such an approach – through a distinct focus on human society – reduces nature to an economic 'dead' space which serves

---

16   Alan R. H. Baker, 'Historical Geography and the Study of the European Rural Landscape', *Geografiska Annaler. Series B, Human Geography* 70-1 (1988): 5-16. For a review of post-phenomenological work in geography see James Ash and Paul Simpson, 'Geography and post-phenomenology', *Progress in Human Geography* 40-1 (2016): 48-66.

17   See for example Mats Widgren, *Bysamfällighet och tegskifte i Bohuslän 1300-1750* (Uddevalla: Bohusläns museum, 1997); Olof Karsvall, 'Retrogressiv metod. En översikt med exempel från historisk geografi och agrarhistoria', *Historisk tidskrift* 133-3 (2013): 411-35.

18   Widgren, 'Can landscapes be read?', 459.

19   Ulf Sporrong, *Kulturlandskapet: människa – landskap – förändring: kulturlandskapsstudier med teoretiska utgångspunkter* (Stockholm, 1983); Margarete Ihse and Helle Skånes, 'The Swedish Agropastoral Hagmark Landscape: An Approach to Integrated Landscape Analysis', in *Nordic Landscapes: Region and Belonging on the Northern Edge of Europe*, eds Michael Jones and Kenneth R. Olwig (Minneapolis: Univ. of Minnesota Press, 2008): 251-80.

20   Richard T. T. Forman and Michel Godron, 'Patches and Structural components for a Landscape Ecology', *BioScience* 31-10 (1981): 733-40.

21   Bjørnar Olsen, *In defense of things: archaeology and the ontology of objects*, (Lanham: Rowman & Littlefield Publishing Group, Inc, 2010): 31; Christina Fredengren, 'NATURE:CULTURES. Heritage, Sustainability and Feminist Posthumanism', 116ff; Camilla Eriksson and Anders Wästfelt, 'Är ett landskap enbart en utsikt? Två frågor i och med införandet av landskapskonventionen i Sverige', *Bebyggelsehistorisk tidskrift* 16 (2011): 90-92.

as a framework but not as an active entity. The physical landscape concept is useful not the least when developed into an integrated perspective, but tends to reduce the human to an ecological factor driving an evolutionary process.[22]

The landscape concept is thus highly complicated, with a range of seldom combined definitions being in use simultaneously. Communication between different 'schools' of landscape is limited by conceptual divides in that the definition of landscape defines the research questions and sets the foundation for the methodology by which those questions are answered. A scenic or perceptual inquiry interprets a landscape radically different from a physical approach although the subject or material itself may be similar. To a certain extent the European Landscape Convention (ELC) deals with this problem through defining landscape as 'an area, as perceived by people, whose character is the result of the action and interaction of natural and/or human factors'.[23] While this widely accepted definition captures some of the complexity of the concept, there is still a tendency to view landscape as a static object of consumption rather than a space which is constantly shaped through human custom, living and use.[24]

In order to bridge the conceptual divide more fully, this article seeks to explore the ways in which different forms of historical landscape interpretation connect in a given area, emphasising the importance of analysing complex relations rather than seeking general patterns. The hope is to increase cross-perceptual communication through this endeavour by illustrating how one landscape concept contributes to another. In order to understand human-environment relations it is not enough to confine an analysis within the borders of a single concept. This paper thus uses the three landscape concepts, as defined by Widgren, in combination, enabling broader interpretations of agrarian historical structures and processes.

The landscape of Östra Frölunda: a case study

The case study was conducted using a combination of physical geographical data, historical maps and ancient monuments in the field, all integrated in a GIS environment. A desk-based study formed the foundation of the analysis, grounded in a retrogressive analysis of the agrarian landscape with focus on the historical maps. The studied area comprised a region in which such studies have been conducted before in combination with archaeological excavation of abandoned fields, which enabled a discussion of land use and settlement history covering a roughly defined period between 500-1800 AD.[25] This period formed the focus of the analysis, starting with an expansive period and ending with the initial stages

---

22 This evolutionary integrated landscape perspective can be found in the work of Ulf Sporrong,: Sporrong, *Kulturlandskapet: människa – landskap – förändring*. However, the evolutionary tendencies still remain in later work, for example Ihse and Skånes, 'The Swedish Agropoastoral Hagmark Landscape'.
23 *European landscape convention = Convention européenne du paysage* (Council of Europe: Strasbourg, 2000); European Science Foundation, 'Landscape in a changing world', 2.
24 Eriksson & Wästfelt, 'Är ett landskap enbart en utsikt?', 91.
25 Catharina Mascher, *Förhistoriska markindelningar och röjningsröseområden i Västsveriges skogsbygder* (Stockholm: Stockholm University, 1993); Pär Connelid, Catharina Mascher and Mats Widgren, 'Länghem – by, huvudgård, kyrka och slitstark trikå', in *Från Stad till Land. En medeltidsarkeologisk resa tillägnad Hans Andersson*, eds Anders Andrén, Lars Ersgård and Jes Wienberg (Stockholm:

of the agrarian revolution in Sweden.[26] The retrogressive analysis is based on a general morphogenetic approach, also building on results from recent years of research in Nordic landscape geography.[27] The physical geographical setting for the analysis was provided by GIS data concerning elevation, soil geology and river flooding which made it possible to relate historic settlement development and land use to the structures of the physical environment.[28] Here a symbolic/ideological perspective is also combined with the physical GIS data through viewshed analysis and observable spatial correlations.

Empirical landscape analysis

The study area of Östra Frölunda[29] is located in south-western Sweden on the western border areas of the South Swedish uplands, more specifically in the valley of the river Ätran, which flows from an area northwest of Ulricehamn to the city Falkenberg on the west coast (Figure 1). The river has developed a meandering pattern in the vicinity of Östra Frölunda, and served as a local border between the hamlets of the area in historical times. Surrounding the river valley is a plateau characterised by a relatively flat terrain crossed by small fissure valleys. The elevation of the area lies between 120-240 meters above sea level which means that it lies above the highest coastline of the latest glacial maximum. While most of the upland region is dominated by till soils, the valley itself consists mostly of glaciofluvial deposits left by a glacial river following almost exactly the course of the contemporary river.[30] To some extent the valley floor also contains postglacial sand and gravel. The contemporary river valley is a well-developed agricultural landscape, dominated by the locality of Östra Frölunda. Most houses and farms are also located in the valley or in comparable settings in the surrounding landscape. Peat bogs, lakes and forest dominates the plateau surrounding the river valley with only a few small islands of agrarian settlement. A similar pattern would have characterised the agrarian landscape of late historical times, where the plateau was mostly used for outland grazing and small scale farming activity. During the Middle Ages and into historical times, an important route called 'Redvägen' followed the river valley and connected the inlands of Västergötland with the west

---

Almqvist & Wiksell International, 2001): 23-34; Pär Connelid, Catharina Mascher, Joachim Regnéll and Eva Weiler, 'Röstorp – tvärvetenskapliga studier av ett röjningsröseområde i södra Västergötland', in *Röjningsröseområden på sydsvenska höglandet. Arkeologiska, kulturgeografiska och vegetationshistoriska undersökningar*, ed Mats Widgren (Stockholm: Stockholms universitet, 2003): 169-206.

26 500 AD coincides roughly with the period which in Sweden is called the Late Iron Age and the Early Middle Ages of continental Europe.

27 For an overview of the development of Nordic landscape geography and its connections to the morphological school, see Mats Widgren, 'Linking Nordic landscape geography and political ecology', *Norwegian Journal of Geography* 69-4 (2015): 197-206.

28 Elevation data was provided by Lantmäteriet (Lantmäteriet GSD-Elevation, Grid 2+), soil geology by Geological Survey of Sweden (SGU) and flooding data by the Swedish National Contingency Agency (MSB).

29 Östra Frölunda is the name of the parish as well as the name of the present locality. The historical hamlet was simply called 'Frölunda'.

30 Glaciofluvial deposits are well drained with high levels of ground water, making them suitable for both travel and cultivation.

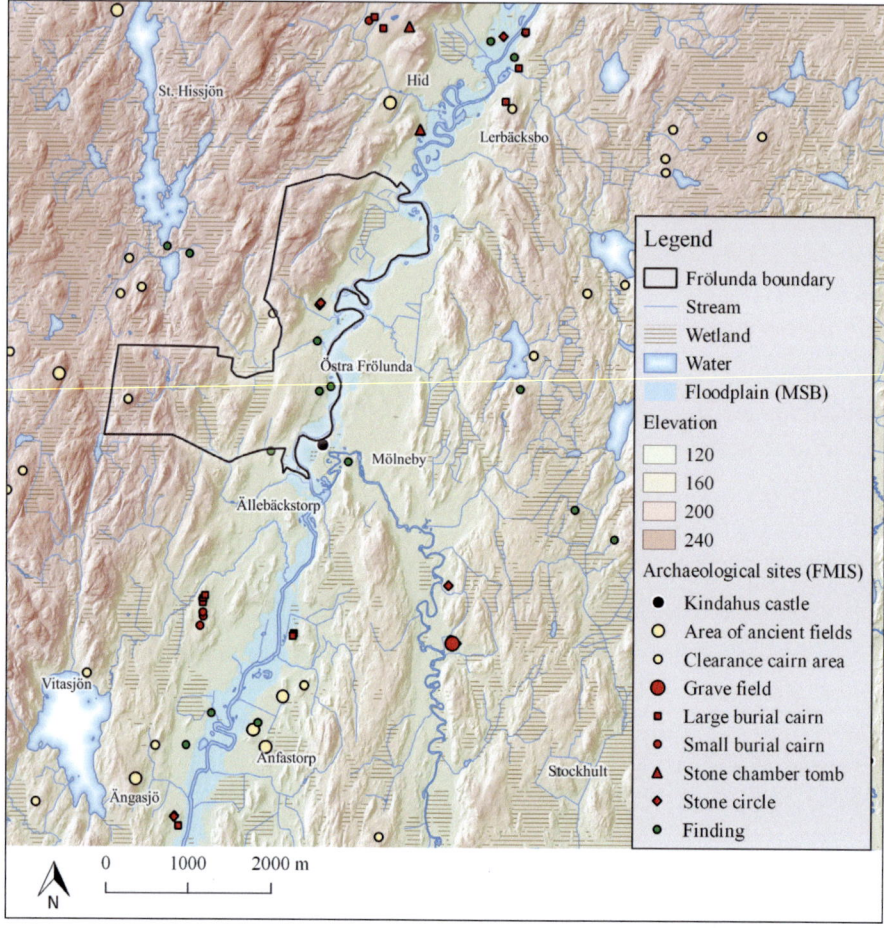

Figure 2. The distribution of archaeological sites in the case study area, where burial cairns represent the Bronze/Iron age periods while stone circles and grave fields more typically dates to the Iron Age. The map also shows the local topography and the historical boundaries of the hamlet of Frölunda as reconstructed from the economic map of the 19th century (RAK J112-25-25, J112-25-20). Data sources: FMIS, GSD-Elevation, Grid 2+ and GSD-Property Map, vector format. © Riksantikvarieämbetet, Lantmäteriet.

coast of Halland (Figure 1). This road served as an interregional communication line and was important from a strategic perspective. Swedish and Danish troops used this road several times during military campaigns.[31]

The historical hamlet 'Frölunda' – which in modern times developed into the current locality of Östra Frölunda – first appears in written records 1396 AD.[32] During the 16th century four farms existed, but a number of archaeological sites suggest that the area has been inhabited and used at least since the Neolithic period.[33]

---

31 Lasse Andersson, 'Borgar och vägsystem: Om några viktiga transportleder mellan Halland och Västergötland', in *Borgar från forntid och medeltid i Västsverige*, eds Berit Hall, Gösta Öborn and Lars-Olof Larsson (Göteborg: Göteborgs arkeologiska museum, 1992): 91-106.
32 *Ortnamnen i Älvsborgs län. D. 7, Kinds härad, 2, Södra delen* (Stockholm: Nordstedt, 1918): 16-17.
33 Among these are several locales with flint flakes, Neolithic stone axes as well as a pot from the early stages of the Late Neolithic.

Two Iron Age stone circles are located to the north of the contemporary community, and small burial cairns can be found on a hill to the south. Traces of past agricultural activity can be observed at several sites with clearance cairns, mostly located in upland locations outside the agriculturally still active river valley. It has been suggested that a majority of clearance cairns in this region can be tied to an extensive form of land use which pre-dates the establishment of permanent field systems,[34] but existing sites can also be connected to small forest farms which existed in the late 19th century, which makes any direct link to prehistoric activity difficult.

The connections between the prehistoric graves of the area and the physical environment suggest that the river valley has been a focal point of human activity at least since the Bronze Age, marked not the least by the large and small burial cairns of the area (see Figure 2.2). These graves are generally aligned with a good view of the valley and the surrounding hills, indicating that although most prehistoric settlements may have been located further uphill, the valley has most likely always served a symbolic and communicative role in local society. The graves and similar structures can not only be seen as religious or symbolic markers in the landscape, but are also signs of ownership manifestation. Through their physical presence in the communicative active river valley, the locals who erected them may have sought to project their ownership rights in the area through kinship.[35]

While the archaeology of the area gives relatively limited information concerning Iron Age activity, early 18th century cadastral maps of the hamlet show clear traces of elder forms of agriculture.[36] The arable in these maps is divided into a form of strip fields which are characteristic of this region, but can also be found in a wide range of contexts in southern Sweden. These strips are generally too broad to be connected to working plots, which has led to the assumption that they are results of land division and planning.[37] Although no trace of these divisions can be found in Östra Frölunda today, field evidence from the region in general suggest that field walls and lynchets have served as barriers marking the strips, which has also enabled radiocarbon dating through excavation.[38] In Kinds *härad*[39], dates have generally been concentrated to 500 AD, but dates from other areas instead point toward 900-1100 AD.[40] It is

---

34 Catharina Mascher ties this extensive land use to the period between roughly 800-0 BC, after which more permanent field systems of strip fields were laid out on the best soils. Mascher, *Förhistoriska markindelningar*. Recent studies have instead emphasised the Roman Iron Age and the High Middle Ages as the most expansive clearance cairn periods, which further complicates this issue. Per Lagerås, 'Agrara fluktuationer och befolkningsutveckling på sydsvenska höglandet tolkade utifrån röjningsrösen', *Fornvännen* 2013 (2013): 263-277.

35 E.g. Jan-Henrik Fallgren, *Kontinuitet och förändring. Bebyggelse och samhälle på Öland 200-1300 e Kr*, (PhD thesis: Uppsala University, 2006) 136-38.

36 Frölunda 1734, LMS O226-8:1, Lantmäteriet; Frölunda 1732, LMS O226-8:6, Lantmäteriet.

37 E.g. Mascher, *Förhistoriska markindelningar*.

38 Mascher, *Förhistoriska markindelninar*; Mats Widgren, 'Strip fields in an Iron-Age context: a case study from Västergötland, Sweden. *Landscape History* 12 (1990): 5-24.

39 A 'härad' is a type of judicial district in which several parishes are included.

40 Mascher, *Förhistoriska markindelningar*; Pär Connelid, 'Byarna kring Falkenberg – Jordbrukslandskapet i Stafsinge, Tröinge och Skrea från vikingatiden till ca 1800', in *Landskap i förändring. Hållplatser i det förgångna*, eds Lennart Carlie, Ewa Ryberg, Jörgen Streiffert and Per Wranning (Ödeshög: Hallands länsmuseer and Riksantikvarieämbetet): 359-98; Mats Widgren, 'Hur drevs den vikingatida – medeltida storgården? Några frågor från Lägerbovada, Ydre', in *Medeltida Storgårdar. 15 uppsatser om ett tvärvetenskapligt forskningsproblem*, eds Olof Karsvall and Kristoffer Jupiter (Uppsala: Kungl. Gustaf Adolfs akademien för svensk folkkultur): 59-72.

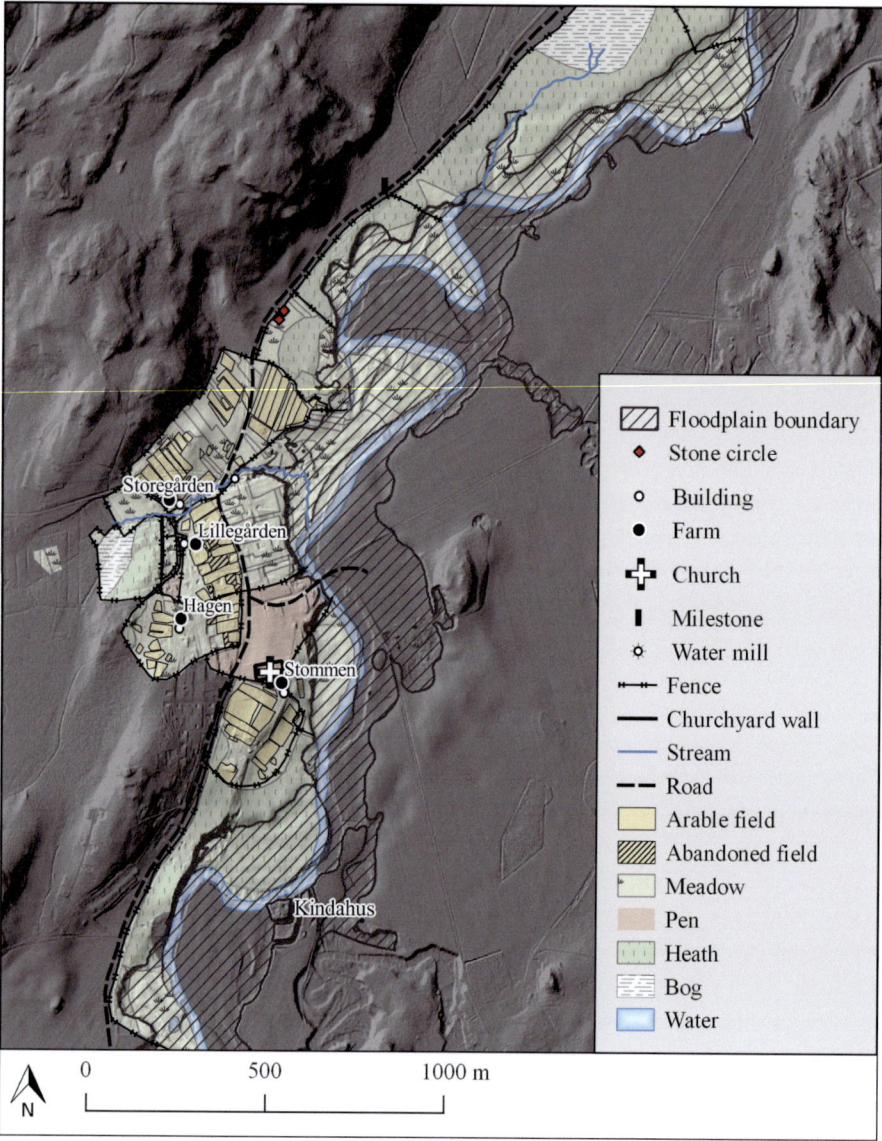

Figure 3. Redrawn version of the 18th century maps of the hamlet of Frölunda, together with the floodplain boundary and the local topography. Data sources: GSD-Elevation, Grid 2+; Updated flood map of Ätran 2015. © Lantmäteriet, MSB.

therefore relatively safe to assume that traces seen in the 18th century maps of the hamlet are the results of land division sometime during the late Iron Age or the initial stages of the Middle Ages. In Frölunda, strip fields seem to appear in contexts where the land was still subdivided between several farms in the 18th century, but also in a large plot of arable which belongs in its entirety to the largest farm of the hamlet, 'Storegården' (Figure 3). This indicates a more extensive previous land division. There are signs that this earlier field system has undergone changes in later periods, shown by the division of strips into shorter parcels of land. Parts of the meadow in connection to the arable is also subdivided in this manner suggesting that the arable has been more extensive in the past – a pattern also repeated in similar contexts in large parts of south-western Sweden.[41]

The layout of the strip fields correlates with the geology of the physical landscape, where strips appear almost exclusively on glacifluvial deposits. Land use during this period was apparently adapted to the physical characteristics of the landscape, where the well-drained glacial alluvium served as a good foundation for arable, while post-glacial alluvium was avoided. This land use relationship is also supported by the flood data from MSB (The Swedish National Contingency Agency), illustrating with clarity to the extent to which the strip fields follow the boundary of the floodplain.

During the Middle Ages, the vicinity surrounding the hamlet of Frölunda was a location of central importance, marked in the present landscape by the foundations of Kindahus castle to the south-east of the hamlet (Figure 3). The road 'Redvägen' passed through Frölunda, and Kindahus controlled this important line of communication, thus playing a strategic role in the political landscape of the period. The castle first appears in the medieval Chronicle of Erik, where a Danish army is said to have laid siege to Kindahus sometime between 1306-1307 AD.[42] Kindahus consisted of three wards – an inner, outer and eastern – each surrounded by dry moats. The moats would fill with water during high flows, while the wards themselves lay protected from water. This strategy greatly improved the defensive traits of the castle, especially during the wetter months of the year.[43] The layout of walls and buildings still remain uncertain as the castle has not been the object of archaeological excavation.

The medieval layout of the hamlet of Frölunda can be roughly traced retrogressively using the historical maps (see Figure 3). As previously mentioned, all four farms found in the maps can be traced back to the 16th century. Three of these farms are described on a map from 1732: Lillegården, Hagen and Stommen.[44] The largest farm on this map, Stommen, is a former rectory, with a large amount of arable and meadow concentrated to a single plot close to the parish church. The arable controlled by this farm to some extent consisted of strip fields, which indicates that the strips at least pre-date the donation of land to the local priest. As previously mentioned, strip fields are usually connected to land division. The arable plot of Stommen being divided into such strips means that it was previously divided between several farms in the hamlet. When the rectory was established, this part of the subdivided arable was donated to the rectory farm. Not all of the lynchets and field walls dividing the strips were removed in this process, resulting in the pattern seen in 1732. A limited amount of new grounds belonging to Stommen has been cultivated at a later date, with no signs of strip divisions.

---

41 Lennart Andersson Palm, 'Boskapsskötseln – en historisk förutsättning', in *Bygden vid ridvägarna – Årtusenden kring Åsunden*, ed Lars Holmén (Borås: De sju häradenas kulturhistoriska förening): 91-106; Per Lagerås et. al, 'Abandonment, agricultural change and ecology', in *Environment, Society and the Black Death. An interdisciplinary approach to the Late-Medieval crisis in Sweden*, ed Per Lagerås (Oxford: Oxbow Books, 2016): 30-68.
42 Sven-Beril Jansson, ed., *Erikskrönikan*, (Stockholm: Tiden, 1985): 116-17.
43 Oscar Jacobsson, Översvämningens landskap, 41-43.
44 Frölunda 1732, LMS O226-8:6, Lantmäteriet.

The map from 1734 describes the farm of Storegården which owns a large and almost entirely non-divided plot of land in the northern part of the main arable fields.[45] This plot is also separated from the rest of the arable by a fence. Storegården should be seen as the principal farm of the hamlet, a relationship most likely established during the High Middle Ages in relation to a wider pattern of social change occurring in Sweden and Denmark during the period.[46] This is supported by the secluded status of the farm, but also by its large revenues in comparison with the other farms of Frölunda. Also, the strip divisions of arable and meadow in this plot are comparatively well preserved, showing limited signs of recent morphological changes, indicating an early establishment of the farm's special status in which there has been little or no cause for changing the established field system. The other farms of the hamlet have used an unregulated open field system where land could be traded and exchanged between farmers;[47] something which over time has caused a previously mixed ownership pattern to evolve into more separately owned plots. Storegården has most likely been moved to the place marked on the 18th century map from a central location in the infields, and land which had previously been divided between several farms was amalgamated under one owner.[48] The agrarian system based on principal farms ended after the Black Death and the Late Medieval crisis, only being preserved in noble and ecclesiastic environments.[49] The settlement and ownership structure seen in 18th century Frölunda thus reflects the results of a medieval development, where many prevailing structures from the Late Middle Ages are still in use while traces of earlier developments have undergone changes.

The annual cropping system of this area from the Late Middle Ages until the mid-19th century required a large cattle stock – and thus extensive meadowland – to produce enough manure in order to sustain the annual cropping of the same fields. Meadow formed a prominent part of Frölundas land use in the 18th century, where a majority of the meadows lay in connection to the river Ätran and inside the floodplain boundary. The surface used for hay production was thus regularly flooded, which contributed to meadow efficiency through a type of natural fertilisation.[50] In the 18th century parts of this old land use system came under threat, marked not the least by the land surveyor's notes. Most of the floodplain meadows were characterised as dry, a pattern also observed in neighbouring hamlets during the same period. Nonetheless, these meadows formed a vital part of the rural system in the area and still produced more hay than meadows outside the floodplain.[51] It is interesting to note that while the ownership of arable strips has started to evolve into more separate plots, the meadows display a more mixed

---

45 Frölunda 1734, LMS O226-8:1, Lantmäteriet.
46 Connelid et al., 'Länghem – by, huvudgård, kyrka och slitstark trikå',; Connelid, 'Byarna kring Falkenberg'; Ericsson, *Terra Mediaevalis*.
47 Karsvall, *Utjordar och Ödegårdar*, 83.
48 Connelid, 'Byarna kring Falkenberg', 393.
49 Ericsson, *Terra Mediaevalis*, 39.
50 Peter Nolbrant, *Vattendrag och Svämplan: helhetssyn på hydromorfologi och biologi* (Solna: WWF); Jacobsson, Översvämningens landskap, 13-14.
51 This phenomenon might be the result of higher ground water pressure, but it can also be assumed that floods with long recurrence periods also contribute to meadow productivity. Similar patterns can be observed in the neighbouring hamlet of Lerbäcksbo: Jacobsson, Översvämningens landskap, 51-52.

ownership pattern. This may be the result of a higher degree of farmer cooperation in meadow land use, but most likely instead reflects the importance of these strips and an unwillingness to exchange certain parcels of land.

It has been argued that floodplain meadows played a vital role in attracting settlements during the Iron Age, as the introduction of certain tools necessary for hay mowing and production in some areas of Sweden coincides with the relocation of settlements to river valleys during the Roman Iron Age (0-400 AD).[52] Others have pointed out that such extensive meadows were not used for hay production until the introduction of the right angled scythe in the Middle Ages.[53] Instead, the hay production was restricted to dry meadows with higher nutrient values during this period. Elsewhere I have argued that floodplains may have served an important function in the production of winter fodder during the climatic decline of the 6th century, where settlements were relocated to locations with better meadowlands.[54] It is thus rather difficult to determine the age of floodplain hay production in the studied area, although the correlation of strip fields with the boundary of the floodplain suggests that natural meadows were either mowed or grazed during the early period of settlement.

Much research in Sweden has emphasised the dynamics of land use over long periods of time, where the layout of arable, hay meadows and grazing grounds have changed historically according to environment, social development, cultural impacts etc.[55] Such dynamics are visible in the map from 1732[56], where parcels of earlier arable in the central field have been transformed into meadow due to poor soil and a degeneration of regular meadowland.[57] Considering the dry character of floodplain meadows the land use change is presumably related to a period of dry conditions occurring between 300-100 BP.[58] Another possibility is that a degradation of ordinary outland pastures in the areas surrounding the valley led to a development in which cattle had to graze long periods on hay producing meadows.[59]

---

52 Peter Skoglund, 'Järn, jordbruk och bebyggelse – sydvästra Småland från romersk järnålder till vikingatid', in *Utmarker, Gårdar och Människor: Om järnålder och tidig medeltid i Sydvästra Småland*, ed Martin Hansson (Växjö: Smålands Museum, 2007): 29-40.
53 Connelid, 'Byarna i Falkenberg', 395.
54 Jacobsson, 'Översvämningens landskap', 74.
55 e.g. Connelid, 'Byarna i Falkenberg'; Aadel Vestbö-Franzén, *Råg och Rön. Om mat, människor och landskapsförändringar i Norra Småland, ca 1550-1700*. (PhD thesis, Stockholm University, 2004); Lagerås et. al, 'Abandonment, agricultural change and ecology'.
56 Frölunda 1732, LMS O226-8:6, Lantmäteriet.
57 The surveyor notes on the parcels in question: 'äro medellst ängens ringheet, som nu dhell med liung förgången är, samt jordmohnens magerheet öde blefne, nyttias till äng, men blifwer ringa gräs i torkåhr'.
58 Rixt De Jong, Dan Hammarlund and Atle Nesje, 'Late Holocene effective precipitation variations in the maritime regions of south-west Scandinavia', *Quaternary Science Reviews* 28 (2009): 54-64.
59 A degradation of outlands has been observed in the neighbouring county of Småland during the 16th and 17th centuries: Vestbö-Franzén, *Råg och Rön*, 191-92.

Themes	Scenery	Institution	Resource
Geology	Flooding	Long distance roads	Geology
Flooding	Long distance roads	Agrarian system	Flooding
Agrarian system	Kindahus castle	Kindahus castle	Kindahus castle
Kindahus castle	Prehistoric graves	Ownership	Agrarian system
Long distance roads		Flooding	Long distance roads
Prehistoric graves		Prehistoric graves	Prehistoric graves
Ownership			

Table 1a. The themes raised by the empirical analysis.

Table 1b. All the themes fitted into the landscape concepts defined by Mats Widgren.

Interpretative perceptual connections

The analysis outlined above contains features that can be connected to a wide range of factors driving historical processes in the study area of Östra Frölunda. Seven different themes can be discerned on which the interpretation has focused (see Table 1a). Based on Widgren's landscape concepts, these fit differently into the three landscape perspectives: scenery, institution and resource (see Table 1b).

The river valley appears to have been a central scenic character, where prehistoric graves are aligned with a good view of the valley floor and the surrounding hills. This seems to indicate that the valley and the river – the importance is emphasised not the least by graves in connection to the floodplain – were topographies with symbolic or ideological values during prehistory. Both Kindahus castle and the church in Frölunda could be seen as scenic continuations of an older religious topographical practice connected to the valley. The castle is interesting in this regard as it was a building which through its presence manifested royal power in the regions bordering the Danish kingdom. The road Redvägen was also part of the symbolical landscape of the valley in that the communicative structure forced an interaction with the riverine landscape while travelling.

Institutional factors in the studied area were active on several administrative levels. The road of Redvägen represented a regional but also national level of communication, the importance of which was physically manifested in the area during the Middle Ages in the form of Kindahus castle. The localisation of the castle can be connected to administrative local structures in the hamlet of Frölunda, seen through the analysis of ownership patterns in the historical maps. These patterns also emphasised the importance of floodplain meadows, which still showed a high degree of land division as opposed to the restructured character of arable ownership. The land use system of the early modern period thus froze some older forms of ownership. As argued above, the prehistoric graves could also be interpreted as a manifestation of ownership and land rights.

The geology of the studied area formed the basis of the resource landscape during the studied period, contributing to the communicative structure of the river valley as well as the foundations for agriculture. The topography of the area in combination with the communicative values of the river valley influenced the localisation of prehistoric graves. Flooding formed a natural part of the landscape

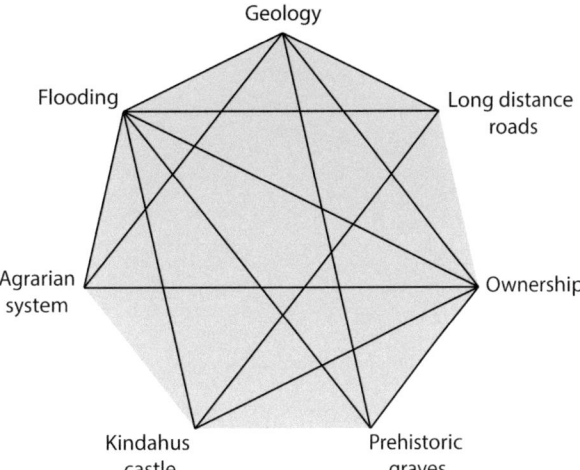

Figure 4. The web of causal relations between the different themes of the empirical landscape analysis.

during the studied period, becoming a vital part of sustaining the agricultural system and potentially attracted settlements during the Iron Age. The soil geology also affected the layout of ownership patterns during this period. Some of the graves were aligned in direct relation to the floodplain and the knowledge of hydrological fluctuations was also used in the layout of Kindahus castle during the Middle Ages. Hydrological dynamics would also have affected the land-based communication of the studied area, especially in presenting a certain danger to structures such as bridges but also to fords and general travelling conditions, regardless of the permeable soil geology.

It should be clear by now that none of the perspectives in isolation captures the full complexity of the study area. Themes appear in several perceptual categories, pointing to an interconnection between different forms of interpretation. The inter-relationships between the themes are illustrated in Figure 4, showing that there is a web of causal connections between different factors active in shaping the studied landscape. Causality between factors is characterised by two-way communication, for example the physical manifestation of ownership through field walls, lynchets etc. affects micro-topographical geology while simultaneously being driven by the geological foundations for agriculture. In Figure 4, the river Ätran and its flooding capacity is connected to all the themes of the empirical landscape analysis, which simply means that by analysing flooding and its related history alone a limited glimpse is gained of the complex landscape relations at work historically in the studied area. Flooding can thus be connected to all the three landscape concepts: scenery, institution and resource. This does not imply that flooding should be seen as the central character of the historical landscape in question, but merely that the relationship between human society and the hydrological dynamics of the physical environment is shaped by a complex reciprocity. Similar arguments could be produced for all themes of the analysis.

It could therefore be argued that the shape, history and continuing relations of landscape in the area surrounding Östra Frölunda are the results of a constant feedback between scenic, institutional and physical factors. In this regard, it is impossible to separate the physical from the symbolic, the institutional from the ideological etc.

Conclusion

This paper has tried to emphasise the diversity of landscape relations in a historical agricultural landscape in south-western Sweden. The cross-conceptual approach enabled a perspective in which the complex connections between different factors in the studied area – as well as the perceptual manifestations of these connections – were illuminated. Landscape relations in the case study area were shaped by a combination of factors which emphasise the interwovenness of human social practice with the physical landscape. Without the combination of different landscape concepts essential factors of this relationship would have been left unstudied.

Most previous studies in this region of south-western Sweden have seen humans as the main actor involved in the shaping of the landscape through social and economic processes.[60] Such an anthropocentric approach remains difficult to maintain in the light of the empirical landscape analysis presented above. Human society naturally still remains an integral part of the historical agricultural landscape which through social interaction and economic needs actively and dynamically reshape the physical environment, but it can no longer be seen as the only actor in an environment which in itself is ever-developing. For example, the riverine factors outlined in this study clearly illustrate a dynamic human-environment interaction in which a multitude of factors shaped the historical landscape relations of Östra Frölunda. The floodplain, shaped by the physical processes of the river, could be seen as an *actant* which through its continuous work – *i.e.* flooding – actively affected the ways in which humans used the landscape. Flooding was a fundamental part of the area's agriculture, and the long-term importance of the floodplain meadows also enforced stability in an otherwise more flexible system of ownership (see above). In the Middle Ages, floods played a role in the defensive layout of a castle and the view of the floodplain was a central part of the prehistoric ritual landscape. Changes in flood frequency or magnitude had the potential to actively affect established relations of the river valley, such as turning floodplain meadows more dry in the 18th century (see above). Such changes have been related to larger environmental variations and to a high degree lie beyond human control (see note 61). A river whose flooding is such an integral part of human-landscape interaction may thus engage in action which in itself infringes on human society.

Building on concepts commonly used in empirical analysis, this perspective could provide a wider platform for discussions regarding historical relations between human agents and non-human actants while simultaneously keeping a close connection to more practical research through the use of an established vocabulary such as different landscape concepts. This would improve the communication between theory and empiricism and enable a fuller cross-fertilisation of ideas, not only in Sweden but also internationally. Theoretical ideas – such as those of the post-human school[61] – could be further explored through this practical engagement with empirical source material. A cross-conceptual approach also confronts the

---

60 E.g. Mascher, *Förhistoriska markindelningar*; Connelid et. al, 'Röstorp – tvärvetenskapliga studier av ett röjningsröseområde i södra Västergötland'.
61 E.g. Fredengren,'NATURE:CULTURES'.

divides currently limiting the practical use of landscape research in dealing with environmental challenges.[62]

Perhaps the foremost example of how this approach could contribute to contemporary practice is the relationship between the floodplain and human society. As was shown in Figure 4, flooding is a complex factor at work in the landscape, involved historically in the construction of society. At present, there is a prevailing antagonistic view on flooding where this naturally occurring phenomenon is perceived as an environmental threat to human settlements and land use.[63] This view is based upon a limited knowledge of how floodplains have coexisted with human society historically, a knowledge gap which can be traced back to the Agrarian Revolution of the 18th and 19th centuries when land was drained and hydrology manipulated.[64] In Sweden, land use and built environments as a result are currently not adapted to withstand the potential but natural threats of flooding.[65] With a historical understanding of the complex relations underlying floodplain and human interaction, it becomes clear that such views cannot be combined with long-term sustainability. Instead future alternatives should be directed towards an adaptation to the dynamics of the physical environment.[66]

This article has merely scratched the surface of the potential involved in using a cross-conceptual perspective in the study of agrarian historical landscapes in Sweden. There is currently a wide range of well-developed methodologies and empirical practices which based on rich and varied source material enables a multitude of research questions. Some of the new questions which can be raised based on the outlined results are: How did the practical interaction between floodplain and human land use shape symbolical or scenic values? In what ways were institutional factors such as ownership affected by climatic variations in precipitation? To what extent were physical landscape changes driven by human symbolical or ideological ideas? These questions all intersect the traditional confines of isolated concepts and can only be answered through a perspective involving a wide theoretical and problematizing approach. The future development of such an approach would clearly benefit the knowledge production concerning the history of agricultural landscapes in Sweden.

---

62 Harden, 'Framing and Reframing Questions of Human-Environment Interactions'; European Science Foundation, 'Landscape in a changing world. Bridging divides, integrating disciplines, serving society', *Science Policy Briefing*, 41 (2010): 6-7.
63 See for example Lloyd Bent, 'Farmers protect their businesses against future flood threat', *The Westmorland Gazette*, December 7, 2016; 'Översvämningar hotar miljarder', *Svenska Dagbladet*, June 14, 2004.
64 Jacobsson, 'Översvämningens landskap', 36.
65 Jacobsson, 'Översvämningens landskap', 75.
66 The concept of Integrated Flood Management is an example of such an approach, which although not historically informed still recognises that it is not enough to work with flood prevention alone. E.g. Wolfgang Grabs, 'Benchmarking flood risk reduction in the Elbe River', *Journal of Flood Risk Management* 9 (2016): 335-342. This approach can be contrasted with approaches advocated in some urban environments, with a stronger focus on environmental engineering. E.g. Oz Shahin, Rodney A. Stewart, Damien Giurco and Michael G. Porter, 'Renewable hydropower generation as a co-benefit of balanced urban water portfolio and flood risk mitigation', *Renewable and Sustainable Energy Reviews* 68-2 (2017): 1076-87.

Acknowledgements

The study was partially financed by funds from Kulturlandskapet's research grant. The author would also like to thank Ådel Franzén for valuable advice and an anonymous referee for very constructive remarks. The paper also benefitted greatly by reviews of Guillermo S. Reher and one anonymous reviewer.

Travel books as landscape archaeology reports

From history to ecological responsibility: The Example of British and American Travellers in the Pyrenees

Francoise Besson[a]

a. Université de Toulouse-Le Mirail, Toulouse, France

Introduction

Travel literature is a protean genre that tells many stories in the guise of autobiographical texts narrating personal experiences. Each personal experience is a pretext for the discovery of places and people seen in the time of the journey but this also gives the traveller the opportunity to have an insight into the history of the place and each stone speaks to the traveller about its history. The description or drawing of castles or bridges shows the evolution of landscapes and thus the apparently autobiographical text becomes at times an archaeological report. Those travel books show readers the transformations undergone by landscapes and lead them from history to ecological responsibility. The example of British and American travellers in the Pyrenees may reveal that dual aspect of travel books. Like archaeologists, travel writers do not content themselves with looking at landscapes with an aesthetic perception; they look for traces, objects and signs telling them about the history of places and the relationship between humans and the landscapes they observe. Travel books can help us to rethink the concept of landscape and landscape archaeology thanks to the observation of traces in the landscape. The example of bridges is significant as they reveal the changes taking place in history and reflected in landscapes. The intermingling of natural features and human constructions reveals historical layers in the landscape, leading the viewer onto ecological awareness.

Can travel books help us to rethink the concept of landscape and landscape archaeology?

Naturalist writer Ann Haymond Zwinger (2000) says that 'to know the world intimately is the beginning of caring' (Zwinger 2000, back cover). This is what travel books suggest. Travel writers' ways of presenting us with human traces or with the non-human world in natural landscapes and with the transformations they perceive, make readers discover geographical areas but those texts have another aim. Travel books may be fundamental in the rethinking of the concept of landscape insofar as they not only show traces of the past in our present landscapes; they also guide readers towards a sense of responsibility and awareness. By showing traces and changes in the landscapes they discover, travellers reveal a new way of considering landscapes, by being aware of the reciprocity they imply between human and non-human worlds. This is what Ann Haymond Zwinger suggests after observing mushrooms: 'Mycelia are like the invisible threads that tie our lives together, ties with family, friends, community, place, country, and to other entities we even don't know about. We may not always know where we are in this complex unity, but we do know the strength of the connections, we're all part of holding the world together. I believe in mycelia' (Zwinger 2000, 39). The traveller's minute observation of the non-human world around her reveals the connections in the human world and between the human and non-human worlds. The landscape is not seen only as a whole but also as a sum of tiny living elements explaining our being in the world. It is the capacity of travellers, whether historians or naturalists, to observe details, that leads them to have a vision of the landscape that is not panoramic but microscopic. And it is that microscopic sense of observation that leads them to have a full view of the complete web. This perception of things is in keeping with Tim Ingold's assertion of the inter-relations between organisms and the environment, between the animate and the non-animate. He explains, in "Temporality of Landscape", that "that generative field is constituted by the totality of organism-environment relations, and the activities of organisms are moments of its unfolding. Indeed once we think of the world in this way, as a total movement of becoming which builds itself into the forms we see, and in which each form takes shape in continuous relation to those around it, then the distinction between the animate and the inanimate seems to dissolve" (Ingold 1993, 164). He goes farther when he adds that "[o]ur actions do not transform the world, they are part and parcel of the world's transforming itself. And that is just another way of saying that they belong to time" (Ingold 1993, 164).

The relationship between the shapes of the land and human eyes implies a dynamic vision of the land in which the eyes perceive changes. This dynamic perception is in keeping with the dynamic vision of nature that appears in an environmental perception of the world. Tim Ingold (2015) says that the word 'landscape' in English, German, Scandinavian languages is not linked with the Greek word 'skopein', to look at, as some researchers thought, but with the notion of 'shape'. He is right to say that it is not directly linked with the eyes but it is linked indirectly with the fact of looking at the land since the notion of shape implies man's way of considering the configuration of what he sees. In the Renaissance, the landscape was defined as 'a part of land seen from the window of one's house' as Yves Luginbühl (1989) says. So even if it is not etymologically linked with the Greek term 'skopein' the notion of landscape is linked with human perception as the shape only exists in relationship to someone who recognizes it as a shape. In Japanese, one of the words for landscape, *Fukei*, is linked with the fact of looking at something: Chihiro Monato says that '*Fukei* [...] reminds us of the presence of a person who is looking at a subject'.[1] So the mere way of regarding the landscape links it with humans through their eyes or their perception of the configuration of a land. Besides, landscapes are constantly transformed according to human constructions and activities, which are different ways of looking at the world; agriculture, plantation or deforestation, urban construction but also historical events like wars transform landscapes.

Travel books, by presenting readers with cities, villages, or natural places, not only show them landscapes as the writers saw them at a precise moment in their own personal existence and at a particular moment of history. They also provide them with a sense of observation of the world suggesting a link between all elements. Thus, their texts and pictures not only take readers towards the past of a place but also lead them to consider their own relationships with any place. Landscape archaeology is a way of finding the observer's link with each landscape. To take an example in a particular mountainous landscape, the Pyrenees provided many Anglo-Saxon travellers with natural or historical elements leading them to a new interpretation of their relationship to the world, which may show a revitalizing of the concept of landscape.

The observation of historical traces in the landscape

The Pyrenean landscape contains traces of the English presence there since the Black Prince's destructive invasion in 1355, and the English occupation of some areas that followed were accompanied by the construction of walled towns (*bastides* in French, a word appearing in a few place-names, like Labastide-Beauvoir, Labastidette and many more). The battles of the Peninsular war from 1808 to 1814 left traces in the Pyrenees, and some towns like Vitoria and San Sebastian, and the Basque Provinces in general bear traces of those battles, as in Northern France the landscape bears the scars of the First World War. Between 1835 and 1840, it was the Spanish civil war that tore the landscape. An English woman traveller, Lady Chatterton, who travelled in the Valley of Aran shortly after the end of the Civil war – her travel book was published in 1843 – observed the sadness of a landscape marked by the traces of war. Travellers read history in the landscape torn by various wars. But it is chiefly the signs of life that they search: they notice objects in the landscape or study place-names, seeing in all those elements the culture of the people living there.

In *Pyrenean Festivals* (1956), Violet Alford, an English ethnologist, evokes inscriptions concerning the history of Pyrenean valleys. Founding her analysis of the Valley of Aran in Spain on the place-name – Aran meaning 'valley' in the Basque language – she looked for traces of the Basque presence in the valley: 'More tangible proof of their occupancy are the discoidal tombstones at Vilamos [...] and the stone at Escunyan (sic) bearing the Euskarian words' (Alford 1956, 96). She also studied the numerous 'round-headed tombstones known as discoidal [...]' (Alford 1956, 263). To reinforce the interpretation of the 'anthropomorphic shape' of those tombstones, she evokes the landscape: 'it is quite true that at twilight a

---

1   Chihiro Minato, Tama Art University, 'Thinking Landscapes'. http://www.midoripress-aeon.net/column/20130702_thinking_landscapes.html, visited May 8, 2017.

rural churchyard seems to be full of dark, round heads peering out of the grass' (Alford 1956, 263). She mingles the 'tangible' reality of the objects and a fantastic vision of the landscape. But she immediately adds a more scientific argument, using the Basque language to reinforce the idea: 'they are moreover called *Gizonak*, men, in the Province of Labourd' (Alford 1956, 263). She not only bases her study on scientific arguments but also seems to find it necessary to immerse herself in the landscape to see it with local people's eyes. She also evokes a 'statue-menhir at *Lugdunum Convenarum*, the remains of the Aquitanian city below St. Bertrand de Comminges' (Alford 1956, 263). She links it to the discoidal tombstones (Alford 1956, 102). The same landscape can give birth to another kind of observation and instead of close-ups on particular objects, a general view of the places suggests that the natural landscape contains the history of the people living there, like agricultural life inscribed in natural and historical landscapes.

An American travel book published in 1923, *Hill-Towns of the Pyrenees*, unveils the travellers' perception of all layers of the landscape and particularly of the importance of agriculture (Oakley 1923). Most general views of villages show, in the foreground, a landscape shaped by agricultural life inscribed in another kind of historical landscape often dominated by a castle or a church with houses around it and mountains in the background: it is as if all the layers of mountain life were visible for the travellers. Two levels of history are inscribed in those engravings: agriculture, which appears as the history of the domestication of plants and animals that has transformed man's life all around the world from the Neolithic; and history at large, representing all the past events defining a people, a city, a country and mankind. The castles and churches dominating villages in those engravings sum up the hierarchical organization of society with a political power represented by the castle and a religious power represented by the church while the houses contain the villagers who are geographically on the lower part of the social ladder as it is represented in the organization of villages. The stone landscape stands for historical society whereas the agricultural landscape represents man's taming of nature. Both are connected in the "temporality of the landscape" as analysed by Tim Ingold. The connection between the natural world and the traces of human work and cultures show "the world transforming itself" (Ingold 1993, 164). That type of representation also reveals the prevailing role of agriculture in rural societies. Thus in the two views of St.Bertrand de Comminges (Figure 1a and Figure 1b), the travellers present their readers with two points of view. The first engraving, which opens the chapter, shows the cathedral from a distance but it is not the dominating element since the man-made building is dominated by the mountains in the background (Oakley 1923, 180). The frame constituted by the two cypresses, trees symbolizing life near graveyards, highlights the presence of the small graveyard in the village at the foot of the hill. Orchards are visible in the distance. The angle of vision shows the embedding of human life and death within nature and in a way it leads us to the awareness of our relationship with the non-human world as the picture shows that all human elements are inscribed in, and dominated by, the mountain. In the second engraving, the stress is laid on the vegetation on the slopes and at the foot of the hill (Oakley 1923, 190): trees evoke wild nature in the middle ground and orchards in the foreground reveal

Figure 1a (left). 'St. Bertrand de Comminges Bears the Proud Head in the Valley of the Garonne"', in Oakley & Oakley, 1923, p. 190. Private collection FB.

Figure 1b (right). 'St. Bertrand de Comminges framed by the cypresses of Saint-Just", in Oakley & Oakley, 1923, p. 180. Private collection FB.

the agriculture in that valley where indeed the cultivation of apple-trees in small orchards was and still is an important element.

The representation of a historical landscape within the natural one and vice versa and the role given to the non-human suggest an environmental perception of things according to Laurence Buell's (1995) criteria:

- 'environmental writing, in contrast to nature writing, assumes the presence of natural history in human history',
- Environmental texts 'open spaces for the nonhuman and its "interests", sometimes privileging a non-androcentred world and its distinct evolution and history',
- 'Environmental writing imports into the text an ethical orientation that makes human beings responsible for the environment and accountable for its health and continuation',
- 'The environmental text assumes the processual order of nature and critiques or avoids a static model of natural change and ecological transformations' (Buell 1995, 7-8).

Perhaps in the environmental perception that appears in many travel books we may be seeing an ecocritical dimension suggesting a revitalizing of the landscape concept. Paradoxically we can find a form of revitalizing in old texts revealing a deep awareness of the relationship between humans and landscapes. Nearly all the general views of Pyrenean villages by Amy and Thornton Oakley show the villages in the distance and in the foreground, there is either a peasant or a shepherd. Everything is shown as being related in those engravings. The low stone walls typical of those mountain regions are always visible: it is not the aesthetic dimension that matters but the life suggested by the landscape that interests the traveller. Two views of a same area, the Capcir, in the Eastern Pyrenees, can show a difference of point of view: a modern photograph on an internet site devoted to hiking[2] presents us with a harmonious view of the place with soft meadows and the mountains in the distance, a quiet village in the foreground. The picture is meant to attract tourists by showing them the quiet beauty of the place. The engraving made by Thornton Oakley in the twenties is different. There are also meadows, the village is in the middle ground and the mountains appear in the distance (Oakley 1923, 98). But what differs is that the foreground is devoted to the work of a couple of peasants with their oxen ploughing a very hard field and the stress is laid on the fact that the field is uneven and sloping, which is reinforced by the caption: 'life is hard in the Capcir'. The two pictures in Oakley (1923) unveil two points of view and also show that times have changed and instead of hard agricultural life, the valley now lives on tourism. The choice in the representations shows that the same landscape reveals the changes that have occurred in the life of the region.

Just as the landscape bears traces of agriculture, history and religion, it also indicates the temporal changes in the area, as they are signalled by the presence of bridges in engravings and photographs.

Iconographical representations of bridges as marks of landscape evolution

The passing from one temporal era to another one is often marked in mountainous landscapes by the superimposition or juxtaposition of several bridges marking several periods in the landscape. The preservation, often for practical reasons, of the former bridge or even bridges when a new one is built, is fixed by artists, painters or photographers, transforming an architectural fact into a visible archaeological text since the viewer can see the different bridges as the reading of different periods, different techniques of construction and also different modes of travels.

Railways in the Pyrenees appeared rather late because of Napoleon wars that had destroyed many places in Southern parts of the country. Thanks to thermal tourism and to the coming of Emperor Napoleon III and his wife Eugenie de Montijo to the Pyrenees, a railway to Tarbes was created in 1859. But most travellers used the road and no railway appeared in the Valley of Aran – which is still the case nowadays – probably as the valley was both completely surrounded by mountains, which made the construction difficult and it was a very poor region. Only a tramway between Marignac (in France) and the Pont du Roy (the frontier between France and Spain, where there was a casino for years) was used between 1912 and 1966. But as there was neither train nor tramway beyond the Pont du Roy, travellers used the road from France.

---

2   http://www.randonades.com/sejours-liberte/randonnee-pedestre/itinerance-en-cerdagne, visited 9 January 2017.

Figure 2. 'Defile near the Bridge of Sia', Joseph Hardy, 1825. Private collection FB.

Figure 3. 'Double Bridge of Sia. Valley of the Gave de Gavarnie', in Thomas Allom, 1841. Private collection FB.

The small wooden bridges allowing the passages of a few travellers in coaches or sedan chairs until the 19th century, were replaced at the end of the 19th and beginning of the 20th century by metal or stone bridges corresponding to the double transformation induced by the increase of tourism and the birth of the automobile.

We have examples with the bridge of Sia by Thomas Allom or on the various photographs where another bridge has been added to the one represented by Allom in 1841 (Figure 3). When Joseph Hardy, in 1825, had represented the same area (Figure 2), he had chosen a slightly different angle of vision, excluding the bridge to keep only the wilderness. Yet the road dividing the mountain already revealed the human presence in the wild area.

Painters (like Thomas Allom or George Barnard) and photographers (Joseph Vigier in 1853, John Stewart in 1857, Louis-Alphonse Davanne in 1864 or Jean Andrieu in 1862-63 and 1868) represented those bridges, as the superimposition of periods and materials was picturesque. Four bridges appear in some pictures after a fourth one was built in 1880.[3] Together with the picturesqueness of the view, these architectural constructions symbolize a link that shows the connexion of people and mountains. With the various representations of the Pont du Roy, the bridge marking the frontier between France and Spain in the Valley of Aran, the juxtaposition of bridges speaks about the evolution of the mountain area. An 18th-century engraving by Nicolas-Joseph Chapuis shows a small wooden bridge whereas the 19th-century engravings by French mountaineer Maurice Gourdon (Figure 4) and Welsh mountaineers Harold Spender and Llewellyn-Smith (Figure 5), show this wooden bridge but beside it, there is a stronger stone bridge suggesting that more people pass the frontier. At the end of the 19th century, in 1895, an even bigger bridge was built, made with the marble from the quarry of Arties, a village in the valley. It was finished around 1925 (Figure 6). Then the traffic increased more and more as the century went by and in 1977, a new Pont du Roy, made of concrete and metal, was inaugurated to usher in a new era with more and more tourists going from France to Spain through the Valley of Aran (Figure 7). The bridges in the mountain landscape as shown by travellers, speak about the evolution of construction, of roads and of tourism. Along with their aesthetic choices, the artists' angles of vision reveal their will to show a place that tells its own history. They sometimes unconsciously unveil the link between the object, the place and human life, which is the aim of archaeology. Landscape archaeology may also appear in the intermingling of nature and human constructions.

Intermingling of nature and human constructions

Many travellers seem to be struck by the similarity they can see between the shapes of mountains and the shapes of architectural ruins. The illustrations in their travel books emphasize this proximity and the rock seems to become a series of layers telling the history of the mountain, from the geological representation of its natural shapes to the constructions of the castles and towers whose ruins speak about a past that has disappeared and is just there in the form of ruins to inform the traveller of

---

3   Several nineteenth-century photographs of those bridges can be seen on this site: http://monuments.loucrup65.fr/pontdesia.htm. Visited 9 January 2017.

Figure 4 (top left). Pont du Roy, 1876, wood engraving by Maurice Gourdon, À travers l'Aran. Private collection F.B.

Figure 5 (bottom left). Pont du Roy, 1897, in Harold Spender and Llewellyn Smith, Through the High Pyrenees. Private collection FB.

Figure 6 (right). Pont du Roy, Beginning of the 20th century, Labouche postcard. Private collection FB. Reserved Rights.

Figure 7. Pont du Roy, 2015, photograph FB.

Figure 8 (top left). Lady Chatterton : « The Ruined Castle of Lordat, on the Road to Ax ». Lithography extracted from The Pyrenees with Excursions into Spain, London: Saunders and Otley, 1843. Private collection F.B.

Figure 9 (right). "The ruined towers of Lordat," in Oakley & Oakley, 1923, p. 165. Private collection FB.

Figure 10 (bottom left). Charles-Richard WELD, 'Olette,' Wood engraving by Pearson extracted from The Pyrenees West and East, 1859.

some remote period. Like the archaeologists unveiling a site and reading life in the ruins they reconstitute into history, the traveller reconstitutes a historical nature. The romanticism of some representations is often an aesthetic mask put on the historical reconstitution of a landscape. Thus, the perfect parallelism between the ruins of castles and the mountains in the engravings by Vicomtesse de Satgé Saint Jean suggests that those mountainous areas were the ideal places for constructions of castles and fortresses as the natural defences of the mountain rock duplicated the architectural ones. It is the same with Lady Chatterton's 'ruined castle of Lordat' (Figure 8) and Thornton Oakley's same landscape (Ariège, Central Pyrenees) (Figure 9) seeming to prolong the mountain. With Charles-Richard Weld's view of Olette (Eastern Pyrenees, 1859), the tower prolonging the castle, the houses, the road and the broken bridge appear as many layers of the human history of the valley surrounded by the wild nature of mountains (Figure 10). And on William Oliver's lithograph representing the village of 'Eaux-Bonnes' in the Low Pyrenees, the stress is laid on the close intermingling between houses and rocks, nature and everyday life, with the Pyrenean people in their traditional dresses appearing as tiny creatures in the majestic mountains. This is also a way of showing the relationship of humans and nature as revealed by the fragility of the human presence in the non-human world, here the mountains, allowing them to live but at the same time reminding them of their place in the world. Representations of the same place may also show the evolution of a landscape.

Thus views of Lourdes castle and the landscape surrounding it represent a span of three centuries. A drawing made by an English aristocrat woman traveller, Lady Fortescue, at the beginning of the 18th century shows the castle as a dominating yet slight human presence within a landscape clearly dominated by nature. An engraving made by Thornton Oakley (1923), two centuries later, shows a different point of view, but things do not seem to have changed a lot except that a road surrounds the hill leading to the castle, suggesting that more people come there. In-between, indeed, there had been the apparitions to Bernadette at Lourdes, bringing millions of pilgrims. But here the travellers did not paint the grotto but the castle, as in the previous centuries; and the road shown leading to it corresponds to the fact that a museum of popular arts and traditions had just opened in the castle in 1921. On recent photographs, we can see how nature not only has receded to be replaced by human constructions but also endemic vegetable species have given way to some palm trees representing plant transfers, as human travel brings about a sort of globalization of vegetation.

Those examples of illustrations in travel books reveal that travel books are interesting documents speaking about the evolution of the Pyrenean landscape. But they can have another function and take an ecological dimension, leading readers to a sense of responsibility.

Travel books as archaeological reports leading to a sense of responsibility and ecological awareness

Travel books may help to answer the question whether the landscape concept can be revitalised by taking a critical look at nature/culture relationships. Their observation of changes in landscapes suggests an ecocritical dimension, leading the way to greater human responsibility towards nature. From the 19th century onwards, travellers were aware of the rarefaction of species and their observation of landscapes revealed an evolution in the living presence in those landscapes.

Hunting was much practised in mountain areas and wild areas in general in the 19th century. It was no ecological problem as long as it was only practised by the indigenous population who killed only enough animals to feed their families. But things changed when English and continental European travellers introduced sports hunting and killed great quantities of wild animals (bears, ibexes, izards and foxes in the Pyrenees) just for fun. This new activity threatened the species and some travellers were aware of that. Some of them had a paradoxical attitude, like Sir Victor Brooke, who hunted and killed so many ibexes that the species completely disappeared from the Pyrenees. Though he was unaware of the damage he did to the Pyrenean fauna, he was shocked because his fellow countryman, Peter Barr, to earn money, had uprooted all narcissi belonging to a rare species in a whole valley.

Yet from the first quarter of the 19th century onwards, travellers showed their concern that some wild animals like the Pyrenean bear were becoming scarcer and scarcer. As early as 1825, Thomas Clifton-Paris was shocked by the worrying disappearance of Pyrenean bears. From the mention of a place-name, 'the Step of the Bear', he thinks about the extinction of a species that gave its name to a particular place: 'The Step of the Bear is some twenty feet across, so Bruin[4] must have been a wonderful beast, a fit inhabitant of this colossal region, which might well be fancied the abode of giants of mighty bone and bold empire [...] Throughout the wild mountains of the Pyrenees, this animal reigns supreme, although of late years, it has become scarce from the extermination war that is waged against it' (Clifton-Paris 1843, 130). Clifton-Paris goes as far as assimilating bear hunting in the Pyrenees to an 'extermination war'. This strong phrase shows that the traveller was aware of the rapidity with which the species might disappear, which unfortunately proved to be true. In a novel published roughly at the same period by an Irish novelist, Thomas Grattan (1825), *Caribert, the Bear Hunter*, the hunting scene is presented from the dog's point of view and the dog is clearly on the side of the hunted animals against the hunters, which shows that Clifton-Paris's worry was no isolated attitude among travellers. Moreover, some more recent travel books speak about the changes due to pollution in the mountains.

At the foot of the highest summit of the Pyrenees, the Aneto peak, there is a beautiful valley, the 'Vallon d'Esserra' praised by all walkers and climbers. Some of the paintings of this once earthly paradise show its evolution and the dangers industrialization brings even to remote mountain areas. Thus Kev Reynolds, a twenty-first century English traveller, mountaineer and author of mountain guide-books and travel books, tells about this Pyrenean area that, when he first visited it and walked in it, was a real garden of Eden (Reynolds, 2004). When he came back there, the valley was metamorphosed. He starts by quoting another traveller who had mentioned the beginning of the construction of a road there in 1897:

> *In 1897 Harold Spender came down the valley of the Esera from its source among the glaciers. In his account of the journey he mentioned this track: 'We passed the baths of Venasque ... and a little below came across some Spanish workmen employed on a road in a desultory fashion. Whether that road will ever be finished is a matter that must rest on the knees of the gods (Spender & Llellyn-Smith, 1898).'*
>
> *Now, as we came to the Baños de Benasque – Spender's baths of Venasque – I saw that the gods had made their decision. Below, on the broad river plain, a contractor's vehicle belched clouds of diesel smoke.*
>
> *Dusk was drawing on by the time we turned the bend into the upper* **sanctuary**, *and we were still on the bulldozed track that had not been there 18 months before. It led deeper into the valley with an urgency I feared. A concrete ford had been created through the river, and where vehicles had used it their skidding tyres had ripped the vegetation on both banks. A* **once-sacred** *meadowland was* **scarred** *with dry mud and the imprints of wheels, not animals. Dwarf rhododendrons had been* **desecrated**, *and rainbow swirls of oil coloured puddles in the track.*

---

4   Bruin is the nickname given by Pyrenean people to the bear.

A sense of foreboding hung over me, and with every step I slipped deeper into a pool of dejection.

Fifty metres from the site of the idyllic terrace on which Keith and I had camped, the rough track finally came to a halt. Three cars were parked there; two Spanish, one French. Cardboard boxes lay strewn among the shrubbery, rotting after a shower of rain. Wine bottles had been smashed against a rock. Toilet paper fluttered from the branches of a pine tree, and tin cans were rusting in the stream.

"Urban motorised man," wrote Fernando Barrientos Fernandez, "has no responsible conservationist regard for nature." […]

"Where," I wondered, "will the izard go to drink now?" (Reynolds: 2013, 21-22, my emphasis)

The colours of the flowers are replaced by the artificial colours of refuse and by the false rainbow polluting mountain water. The 'once-sacred meadowland' is now 'scarred' and this near anagram sums up the situation and the message: the sacredness of nature is literally scarred, irremediably wounded by the 'Urban motorised man.' The frame of quotations also sums up the shift from the beginnings of the construction of mountain roads, and the result nearly a century later. For profit motives, 'the valley's innocence' had been 'betrayed'. The strong words used by the mountaineer are meant to urge the reader to revolt, to become aware of the destruction of mountain areas by the construction of roads meant to bring more tourists. The description of the evolution of the landscape becomes a way of urging readers and walkers to a sense of responsibility. He shows us that as tourists, we are responsible for this evolution, but as mountaineers, aware of our responsibility, we have a duty to prevent the mountain landscape from being polluted and destroyed by our human presence. The depiction of the evolution of the landscape is an active one showing that texts as landscape archaeology reports may also be ecological manifestoes meant to suggest the human role in the future through man's role in the past. Before ending his chapter, the mountaineer writes: 'Up in the Maladeta's slopes a shepherd's campfire glowed like a beacon. The glaciers were barely perceived, yet a shadowy profile against distant snows announced that the mountains still remained.' (Reynolds: 2013, 22). The mountain remains but all the terms suggesting an ominous future, like 'foreboding' are meant to draw the reader's attention to the necessity of preventing that kind of transformation from destroying the 'beauty' of mountains, their 'innocence', their 'sacredness', that is to say, simply their life. The text ends on a question about an izard, the izard which, eighteen months before, the mountaineers had seen while he was drinking in the clear stream. The stress laid on the pollution of the place shows that it is mountain life as a whole that is threatened.

Conclusion

The connexion between the genre of the travel book and the geographical area, mountains, is perhaps one of the explanations why travel books may at times play the role of archaeological reports revitalizing the concept of landscape. Mountains are probably the natural space that leads travellers and mountaineers to see more clearly than other areas the relationship between the human world and the landscape, as mountain villages are not separated from the mountains; they are integrated into them and mountain landscapes suggest that nothing is separated: human constructions cannot be separated from the natural world, which reminds us that the human must not be defined in opposition to the non-human but in close connection with it. Moreover, travel books, which belong to a particular literary genre, may be written by literary writers as well as scientists and whoever the writers are, they devote their pages to a representation of the landscapes they want to show their readers that is as precise as possible. Being curious, travellers become researchers, trying to make the link between the landscape and the people living in the area, their languages, everyday life, history, whatever composes the life of a place. Because travellers can see the link between the human and the non-human, humans and landscapes, their own awareness of this connexion leads to readers' awareness of their own relationship both with the human other and with the non-human other. This is where the travel book revitalizes the landscape concept: travel books look for traces of the past in various geographical areas and so doing they suggest a new way of conceiving our relationship with landscapes. The traces of the past seen in landscapes and described in travel books throw light on man's way of tackling the future. Travellers have the sense of observation in common with archaeologists. Instead of digging into the soil in search of what is hidden in the landscape, they will dig into the visible world to try to find all the implications of the landscape they can see. Scott Slovic, in his book *Seeking Awareness in American Nature Writing* (1992), prolonging what the American writer Wendell Berry said, writes: 'The place [Berry] says, "will reveal its secrets to the human observer, but it takes prolonged contact: the only condition is your being there and being *watchful*" (Slovic 1992, 169- (my emphasis). This necessary watchfulness is enhanced by the process of writing' (Slovic 1992, 12-13).

It is that watchfulness opening on awareness that archaeologist Jacquetta Hawkes underlines in *The Land*. At the moment of her death, Mel Gussow, the journalist paying a homage to her, reminded us of what she said when discovering a Neanderthal skeleton: "I was conscious of this vanished being and myself as part of an unbroken stream of consciousness."[5]

It is that consciousness of being "part of an unbroken stream of consciousness" that travellers reveal through watchfulness that may transform mere landscape observation as sight-seeing into landscape perception as the deep image of the human relationship with the world, an image found in the multiple layers of the landscape that give us all the elements that are necessary to become aware of our relationship with landscapes and with the non-human world. The consciousness of the beauty of the world and of our belonging to the world can be read in any tree, in any plant, in any thicket. As Jacquetta Hawkes writes: "The answers to all the great secrets are hidden somewhere in this thicket, those of ethics and aesthetics, as well as of metaphysics (Hawkes 3).

---

5   Jacquetta Hawkes, quoted by Mel Gussow, "Jacquetta Hawkes, Archeologist, Is Dead at 85," in *The New York Times*, March 21, 1996. https://www.nytimes.com/1996/03/21/arts/jacquetta-hawkes-archeologist-is-dead-at-85.html.

Acknowledgements

The paper benefitted greatly of reviews of Guillermo S. Reher and one anonymous reviewer and the author would like to thank them for the roads they opened to her.

References

Alford, V. 1956. *The Singing of the Travel*, London: Max Parrish.

Alford, V. 1937. *Pyrenean Festivals*, London: Chatto and Windus.

Buell, L. 1995. *The Environmental Imagination*. Cambridge, Mass. London: The Belknap Press of Harvard University Press.

Chatterton, Lady H.G. 1843. *The Pyrenees with Excursions into Spain*, 2 vol., London: Saunders and Otley.

Clifton-Paris, T. 1843. *Letters from the Pyrenees*, London: John Murray.

Duloum, J. 1970. *Les Anglais dans les Pyrénées et les débuts du tourisme pyrénéen (1739-1896)*, Pau: Les Amis du Musée Pyrénéen.

Fortescue, Lady H.A. 1996. Carnets de dessins, in Pierre Tucoo-Chala, Joseph Ribas, Hélène Saule-Sorbé (ed). *Lady Fortescue, une aristocrate anglaise aux Pyrénées en 1818*, Toulouse: Editions Loubatières.

Fourcassie, J. 1940. *Le Romantisme et les Pyrénées*. Paris: Gallimard.

Gaston, M. 1975. *Images romantiques des Pyrénées, Les Pyrénées dans la peinture et dans l'estampe à l'époque romantique*, Pau: Les Amis du Musée Pyrénéen.

Grattan, T. 1825. Caribert, The Bear Hunter, *In High-Ways and By-Ways or Tales of the Roadside picked up in the French Provinces by a Walking Gentleman*, London: G. and W. B. Whittaker (second series), 212.

Gussow, M. 1996. "Jacquetta Hawkes, Archeologist, Is Dead at 85," in *The New York Times*, March 21, 1996. https://www.nytimes.com/1996/03/21/arts/jacquetta-hawkes-archeologist-is-dead-at-85.html, accessed 4 February 2020.

Hardy, J. 1825. *A Picturesque and Descriptive Tour in the Mountains of the High Pyrenees…*, London: Ackermann.

Hawkes, J. 2012. [1951]. *A Land with an introduction by Robert MacFralane*, Collins Nature Library.

Ingold, T. 2015. *Critical Landscapes. Art, Space, Politics*, ed. by Emily Eliza Scott and Kirsten Swenson, Oakland: University of California Press.

Ingold, T. 1993. "The Temporality of the Landscape," In *World Archaeology*, Vol. 25, No. 2, Conceptions of Time and Ancient Society (Oct., 1993), 152-174. http://www.jstor.org/stable/124811, accessed 4 February 2020.

Luginbühl, Y. 1989. *Paysages, représentations des paysages du Siècle des Lumières à nos jours*. Paris: éd. La Manufacture.

Macfarlane, R. 2012. "Re-Reading: A Land by Jacquetta Hawkes," In *The Guardian*, 11 May, 2012. https://www.theguardian.com/books/2012/may/11/rereading-a-land-jacquetta-hawkes, accessed 4 February 2020.

Oakley, A. & Oakley, T. 1923. *Hill-Towns of the Pyrenees*, New York: The Century Company.

Oliver, W. 1843. *Scenery of the Pyrenees*, London: Colmaghi and Puckle.

Pratt, M.L. 1992. *Imperial Eyes. Travel Writing and Transculturation*, Londres : Routledge.

Reynolds, K. 2013. *A Walk in the Clouds*. Fifty Years Among the Mountains, Cumbria: Cicerone.

Reynolds, K. 2004. *Alpine Points of View*, Cumbria: Cicerone.

Russell, H. 1888. *Souvenirs d'un montagnard* (1858-1888), Pau: imp. Vignancour.

Saule Sorbe, H. 1993. *Pyrénées voyage par les images*, Serres-Castet: Editions de Faucompret.

Slovic, S. 1992. *Seeking Awareness in American Nature Writing. Henry Thoreau, Annie Dillard, Edward Abbey, Wendell Berry, Barry Lopez*, Salt Lake City: University of Utah Press.

Spender, H. & Llewellyn-Smith, H. 1898. *Through the High Pyrenees*, London: Sampson, Low, Marton and Company.

Weld, C.R. 1859. *Pyrenees West and East*, London: Longman, Brown, Green, Longmans and Roberts.

Zwinger, A.H. 2000. *Shaped by Wind and Water. Reflections of a Naturalist*, Minneapolis: Milkweed Editions, Credo collection.

Fragments of the Wild: Wordsworth's Yew Trees and Contemporary Archaeology

Andrew Hoaen[a]

a. Institute of Science and the Environment, University of Worcester, Worcester, United Kingdom

'The roots and the springs of the valley were always wild…' (Le Guin 1985:52)

Introduction

Trees, and in particular veteran trees, are long lived organisms of the world around us. They come in many shapes and sizes with around 30 native species present in the UK (Rackham 1990). Trees and their associated woods have been the subject of many investigations in environmental history (*e.g.* Rackham 1990, Peterken and Game 1984, Watkins 2014). However, until relatively recently the study of archaeological landscapes has not involved recording trees (cf. Barnes and Williamson 2001, Mills 2013, Handley and Rotherham 2013). Within environmental and landscape archaeologies the 'natural' world, both domestic and wild, is poorly theorised and poorly integrated into wider syntheses (Cummings and Whittle 2003, Plumwood 2006, Richer and Geary 2017, Hoaen n.d.). At the time this research was conducted the idea that archaeologists should make veteran trees the centrepiece of an analysis appeared quite an experimental idea. Although the archaeology of the contemporary or the recent past was well established (cf. Buchli and Lucas 2002a, Harrison and Scholfield 2009, Graves-Brown et al. 2013a) this methodology had not been extended to the study of the natural world. In archaeology, even a search in Google or Google Scholar on the term 'contemporary environmental archaeology' does not produce any direct hits. The aim of using an environmental humanities framework in this case study is to bring elements of the previously ignored natural world into cultural landscape frameworks and allows a better understanding of how environments come into being and landscapes come to be perceived.

Veteran trees as defined by Natural England (1999) are individual organisms in the landscape, that can live to a great age; an average oak of around 3.5m to 5.0m girth (1 – 2m in diameter) will range from 250 – 500 years old. Such trees may have grown up as 'wild trees' or by deliberate planting. Trees whether planted or wild may have been managed in some form or other over the course of their long lives. It is this management aspect that has led to the production of recent

Figure 1. Photo of Yews.

government guidance that veteran trees should be considered as *"Archaeological relicts"* because *"their age and structure are often a result of past human use"* (POST 2014:1). Ingold in his paper the Temporality of Landscape argues that trees are an integral part of human-environment interactions;

> *"In the case of the tree, we have already observed that its growth consists of the unfolding of a total system of relations constituted by the fact of its presence in an environment…and that people as components of the tree's environment play a not insignificant role in this process" (Ingold 1993:170).*

This study assesses the ubiquity and applicability of a contemporary archaeological approach to the study of trees and wilds in their environmental setting. It uses a case study centered on a yew grove, located in the side valley of Seathwaite in the English Lake District (Figure 1). These trees, known collectively as the 'Fraternal Four', were commemorated by the English Nature poet Wordsworth in his poem 'Yew Trees' (Curtis 1983). Drawing on a range of past and present poets and thinkers the paper will embed its theoretical approach to the wild within the field of the environmental humanities and philosophy (*e.g.* Snyder 2010, Thoreau 2000, Leopold 1968). Finally, contributions of philosophers such as Plumwood (2006) and Woods (2001) along with ecocritics such as Bate (1991) and Garrard (2004) will be considered.

While most tree species in England are not domestic, they are an odd category, inasmuch as they are wild but cultivated; therefore, they confound the tidy definitions that scientists and heritage managers try to create for them in England (Watkins 2014, Hoaen n.d., Hay Festival 2015). As archaeologists and palaeoecologists, we examine the remains of tree pollen, charcoal, and wood, found in sediments but we seldom consider the living organisms as a record of past and contemporary environments. One area in which investigations on still standing trees do occur is in modelling and experimental work (Edwards et al. 2015, Gaillard, et.al 2008). Trees as components of woods have long been studied as part of wider environmental histories, particularly in Britain (Rackham 1990, Peterken and Game 1984, Rotherham 2011). But whilst an archaeological approach to the physical remains of banks and structures in woods has often been taken, using an archaeological approach to the trees themselves has rarely been done by archaeologists and ancient trees are rarely recorded in UK Historical environment records (however, trees in the landscape are studied by landscape historians and historical ecologists see Muir 2006, CBA 2016, Barnes and Williamson 2011, Mills 2013, POST 2014).

Towards a contemporary environmental archaeology

In 2002 Buchli and Lucas laid out the reasons behind, and suggest ways forward, for investigations of the archaeology of the present day and recent past (2002b). As a new and relatively reflexive field, updates on progress and new ways of delivering the original aspirations have been frequent. As such it has been relatively straightforward to monitor the expansion of interest into new areas including *e.g.* graffiti archaeology and conflict archaeology (Harrison and Scholfield 2009, Graves-Brown, et al. 2013b). Despite the new interest in 'things' in archaeology and other disciplines as part of the material turn (*e.g.* Miller 2010) and the rise in interest in assemblages and the agency of non-humans (Hamilakis and Jones 2017), practitioners in this field rarely extend the approach of contemporary archaeology to the natural world or the organisms within it. For example, in the recent Oxford Handbook of the Archaeology of the Contemporary World (eds. Graves-Brown et al 2013) none of the papers deal with the environment and the non-human except obliquely, and few of the papers acknowledge the wider environments in which humans live and upon which they depend for their sustenance. A notable exception is the article by Holtorf on animals in zoos (Holtorf 2013), although its value is limited because it does not engage with environments outside of the zoo.

As part of their manifesto, Buchli and Lucas (2002b, 4) quote Rathje (1979):

> "*archaeology ... is 'a focus on the interaction between material culture and human behaviour, regardless of time or space'.*"

They argue that archaeological work in the present falls into two broad camps, those whose aim it is to inform the past through a study of present day behaviours, and those in which the purpose is to look at the present through the lens of longer term behaviours of humans.

One of the key areas identified by Buchli and Lucas is that of the unconstituted, that is, those parts of the present that are hidden from view and which are in some senses suppressed (op. cit.:13). I would argue that large parts of the natural world, both living and non-living, have been removed from the archaeological discourse. We, archaeologists are not comfortable with the concept of nature, and so an anthropocentric approach has grown up in which humans are the centre of all analysis (Miller 2010).

Rathje argues that a contemporary archaeology should involve the recording of material traces of human activity in both the 'cultural' and 'natural' environments in which human actions occur (Rathje 2002). Rathje goes on to say that one of the advantages of studying the material culture of the present day is that it allows us to check that people are actually doing what they believe and say they are doing (op. cit.:64). A contemporary environmental archaeology that seeks to build on this work will look at present day habitats and try to understand their ecological and cultural basis, recognising that such environments exist on a continuum from highly managed conifer plantations and nature reserves to unmanaged veteran trees and abandoned fields and woods. In keeping with a contemporary archaeology, such studies should be interdisciplinary in nature (Harrison and Scholfield 2009).

What is beyond the bounds?

The English upland landscape is traditionally divided into two areas – the cultivated land of the valley floor and the 'waste' of the valley sides and fells. The cultivated areas and the 'waste' of the common land are often separated by a 'ring garth', a stone wall that encompasses the valley (Edmonds 2004). Although often described as 'waste', the valley sides and fell tops are an important source of materials for grazing, timber, fodder, fuel etc. (Edmonds 2004). It was the 'waste' 'beyond the bounds' that was traditionally viewed as wilderness within accounts of the British landscape (Hoskins 1969, Watkins 2014). This everyday definition of wilderness and wild derives from the Anglo-Saxon *wilde*. The term is first recorded in AD 725 and means a plant, animal or human that is not tame or domesticated, and a place or a region which is uncultivated or uninhabited. Hence '*wildeornesse*' or wilderness where the wild beasts live beyond the bounds of cultivation (Garrard 2004, OED 2017). In its original meaning waste and wilderness are not concepts associated with the concept of a pristine nature rather they are part of continuum from wild (i:e unmanaged to cultivated ground) see recent discussion by Peterken (2019) of meaning of natural in regard to British woodland, and Hoaen (2019a, 2019b).

There is a wide literature in historical ecology dealing with issues of pristine wildernesses, however, this short discussion will focus on how that debate has manifested in the environmental humanities.

The concept of what has become known as the received idea of wild and wilderness (*sensu* Woods 2001), the American National Park Service (1964) act of definition of a wilderness as a vast space which is pristine i:e has not been disturbed by man. This concept of the pristine wilderness has become highly contested, especially within the arenas of North American conservation, environmental history and philosophy (Oelschlaeger 1991, Callicott and Nelson 1998 and papers within, especially Guha and Bear and Luther). An argument has developed of wilderness denial (Woods 2001). There are two main oppositional groups to the idea of wilderness the first led by the political right wing 'Wise Use Movement', whose goal is to sell off federal land in the US so that it can be placed in private ownership for development (Snyder 2010), and a second group comprised of a coalition of Native Americans (Bear and Luther 1998), indigenous peoples across the world (Guha 1998), and influential thinkers such as Callicott and Nelson (1998), who also deny the possibility of a wilderness condition. The denial of wilderness largely depends on arguments relating to the purity and pristineness of wilderness areas. The argument against is that many of these areas have been utilised by non-European groups long before their designation as wilderness and so cannot be considered pristine (Callicott and Nelson 1998a). Native Americans and Australian aboriginals were often forcibly deprived of their land to create these "pristine" reserves and have consistently had their land claims rejected, so there is an aspect of environmental justice in the privileging of nature over the claims of the original human inhabitants (Bear and Luther 1998, Guha 1998, Plumwood 2006, Dalglish 2012). A third argument against wilderness is that of scale; outside of North America few places are of a size to be declared wilderness areas as they are understood in that continent (*e.g.* NPS 1964, Ralston 2004, SNH 2014, EU 2016).

Opponents of this pristine view of the wilderness model argue that the purity challenge to wilderness is problematic (Woods 2001). They would argue that wilderness can continue to exist after disturbance and that it is the degree of management that determines a wilderness or a wild condition, a view that is shared by public surveys of wilderness (SNH 2014). Furthermore, Plumwood suggests that this represents a male and sexist view of nature as a feminised possession in that it must remain unsullied to maintain value (1993, 2006). Snyder, in a poetic argument writes that nature (wilderness) will grow afresh from each new disturbance but still remain wild (2010). There is not space here to discuss the concerns of the environmental justice movement but see Plumwood (1998, 2006) and Woods (2001).

There has for some considerable time been an ongoing debate about what the original state of vegetation and woodland would have been in Holocene Europe as a result of the Vera hypothesis (Vera 2000 and see recent papers in British Wildlife Alexander et al. 2019 and Fyffe 2019). These demonstrate that neither past ecologies nor the interpretations of them are static through time. An alternative way of looking at disturbance and regeneration is to consider it as a continuum from cultivated to wild or as Peterken (2019) argues for British woodlands from managed to semi natural to natural, rather than as a series of essentialist states.

As archaeologists, we have rarely been involved in these theoretical debates in the environmental humanities (though see Simms 1992, Ralston 2004, Dalglish 2012, Hoaen 2019a, Hoaen 2019b). Nevertheless, there are signs that this may be beginning, with the growth of interest in non-human worlds as described by actor-network theory (Latour 2005), assemblages of vibrant things (Bennett 2009, Hamilakis and Jones 2017) and phenomenological perspectives of being in the world (Ingold 2000). Archaeologists, as discussed earlier, have tended to study environments either from the technical viewpoint of past species assemblages or resources (O'Connor and Evans 2005), or as static backdrops against which human action takes place (Tilley 1994).

It seems appropriate, therefore, to examine how debates in the environmental humanities and human geography may help with archaeological interpretation of areas 'beyond the bounds'.

Urban wilderness

There has been a renewed interest in 'wild spaces' in human, particularly urban, geography (Jorgenson and Tylecote 2007, Whatmore and Hinchcliffe 2010, Lorimer 2015). The following section will explore some of this literature as it pertains to scale in the environment, the balance between the wild and cultivated and the processes that come to dominate across time and space beyond the bounds. In their review of urban wild spaces Jorgensen and Tylecote make several interesting points about the way in which nature has come to colonise urban brownfield sites. As many of these sites are small often less than a hectare they make the point that wilderness (and to a lesser extent the related concept of woodland) have a *'role as psychological and social (or rather asocial) territories as well as geographical ones'* (Jorgenson and Tylecote 2007:445). In their recent book Edgelands, Farley and Roberts attempt to catalogue these new hybrid ecologies in England (2012). They make the point that wilderness in England is often to be found as much in small neglected sites on the outskirts of cities as it is in the carefully curated areas of nature reserves and national parks.

The role of urban brownfield sites as new, contemporary small scale wilds and wildernesses has also been highlighted by Whatmore and Hinchcliffe (2010), in their study of 'feral spaces' in Bristol. Here they highlight the way in which such spaces provide a refuge from the city for the local inhabitants. Using the example of Royate Hill, an abandoned stretch of railway line (now a nature reserve) they discuss how such *'ecological landscapes'* come into being and their importance not just to the local inhabitants but also as wildlife refuges. Similarly, Lorimer (2015) highlights the importance of urban ecological regeneration and habitats for rare invertebrate species. An excellent example is the UK's first *'Brownfield rainforest'* at Canvey Wick on Canvey Island, which was listed as a Site of Special Scientific Interest (SSSI) in 2005 (Vidal 2003).

In these studies, scale in the definition is unimportant; what is important in defining these places as wildernesses or wild places is a combination of the lack of ongoing human management allowing 'wild' successional processes to dominate, and a sense within the local community that the space is a wild space, which can be used for recreation or for other more subversive activities. This psychological and social aspect can of course be either positive as a place to walk or it can be negative as a space associated with fear (Tylecote and Jorgensen 2007).

Ecocriticism, Wordsworth, Thoreau and the wild

The development of ecocriticism in English Literature can be said to begin with the publication of Johnathan Bate's influential book *Romantic Ecology* (1991) a study of Wordsworth as a nature poet and proto-ecologist (Garrard 2004, *cf. the earlier Country and the City Williams 1973*). Nature, wilds and wilderness have been of long standing interest to environmental philosophers and writers (Coletta 2001, Thoreau 2000, Muir 2008, Naess 1995, Snyder 2010). For Wordsworth, nature could be divided into that which he associated with the domestic sphere of the home farm and its fields and the more remote nature of the high fells and moors of his native Cumbria (Garrard 2004). He was predominately a pastoral poet, though as Bate suggests he was also a poet with an interest in what later became known as ecology (1991). Subsequently, he inspired the American authors Emerson and Thoreau.

Thoreau differs from later writers on the wild, such as Muir and Leopold, in his awareness that wild and nature are contingent on local histories. He does not need purity and vast scale to recognise the wild and the nature within it. In his sojourn at Walden, Massachusetts, he recognised the secondary nature of the woods in which he was staying, and the presence of indigenous farmers' artefacts in the soil he tilled (Thoreau 2000). The wild for Thoreau, I would argue, is part and parcel of human experience. However, whereas in the past it was uninhabited or partially inhabited and used for essential resources such as grazing, fuel, bedding etc., Thoreau transforms it so that the wild is now also essential for wellbeing and peace of mind. It can be argued that Thoreau restores the concept of the wild as a place for contemplation and renewal an approach potentially analogous to that of earlier Christian monastic thought (cf. the nature poetry of early Celtic monks, Jackson 1971).

Spence (1999) has drawn attention to the way in which wilderness took on a more austere bureaucratic dimension that ignored or undervalued aspects of Thoreau's thought after his death. This rejection of human presence and the need for purity in the wild consequently deprived Native Americans of their homes in the nineteenth and twentieth centuries (Spence 1999). Garrard, in his chapter 'Wilderness', summarises how this purity trope came to dominate thinking both among nature writers and poets but also conservation movements in the twentieth century (2004).

Feminist philosophers, particularly Plumwood (1993, 2006) and Soper (1995), have been critical of this development in twentieth century wilderness thought. They are joined by the poet and thinker Gary Snyder who, using the metaphor of Artemis and the spring, argues *contra* Leopold that the wild and nature are endlessly creative, and that the wilderness condition can spring up again, renewed. This can be seen in Wordsworth's poem 'Michael' which recounts the economic failure and death of the Shepherd Michael. In this poem Michael's cottage is destroyed by the plough. A sheepfold he was building is reduced to an unrecognisable pile of stone, covered in vegetation (Curtis 1983).

The case study: Borrowdale Yews, Archaeology and places beyond the bounds

The Borrowdale Yews are thought to be over 1500 years old (Pankhurst 2014) and are located at NY236125 at an altitude of approximately 150m in the small side valley of Seathwaite at the end of Borrowdale in the English Lake District (Figure 2). This is the uncultivated valley side above the River Derwent. The valley has been repeatedly glaciated and has a rugged character with steep sides that are used for woodland and rough grazing. Previously, graphite mining took place locally, along with a range of traditional woodland industries such as charcoal burning and coppicing. Little arable farming has occurred in the valley due to the edaphic and climatic constraints (the valley has the highest recorded rainfall in England, at over 5m per annum), and the end of the valley is heavily shaded and unsuitable for arable agriculture (Ratcliffe 2002, Scholfield 2007). Descriptions of the valley range from early travellers such as Thomas Gray, for whom the path over Styhead Tarn was too intimidating and where "the reign of Chaos and Old night" occurred (Lindop 2015), to present day heritage professionals for whom the valley is a 'cultural landscape' (LDNPA n.d.).

Wordsworth wrote his poem 'Yew Trees' in 1803 and subsequently published it in 1815 (Curtis 1983, Fulford 1995). Ruskin regarded it as one of the finest pieces of nature writing. Although Wordsworth did not include the Yews in his own

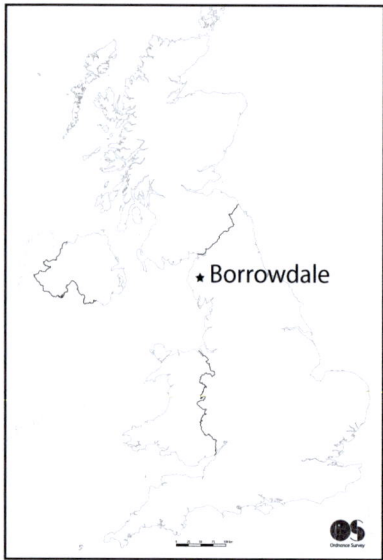 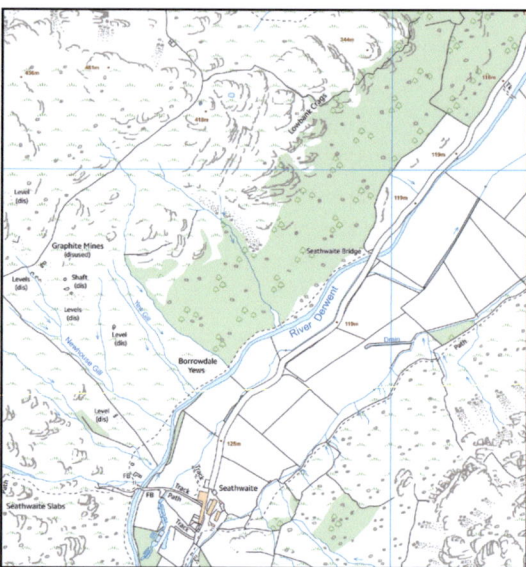

Figure 2. Location of Borrowdale Yews (Use under licence from Digimap 2017).

guide (Wordsworth and Bicknell 1984), the trees subsequently became part of the tourist itinerary for visitors to Borrowdale (Lindop 2015). From the middle of the nineteenth century onwards they have been the subject of numerous paintings and photographs, and the poem and the trees now have their own small bibliography. Of most interest to this study are a series of photographs and engravings from the mid to late 19th century held by the Wordsworth Trust in Grasmere. A photograph (GRMDC.KA5.51 (anon)) record the grove as four trees before the hurricane of 1883 (Rawnsley 1884). The trees suffered crown loss in this storm and one of the Yews blew over, and though the felled tree was recorded as undergoing regeneration subsequently, none of these saplings survived (Fulford 1995).

The tree's girths as measured by Hindson (2012) in 2003 are as follows.
- Yew 1 6.73m; in 1847 it measured c.6.40m (Gilks and Gilks 1847)
- Yew 2 fallen trunk 3.15m
- Yew 2 standing trunk 4.65m
- Yew 3 4.52m
- Yew 4 fallen trunk; Hindson (2012) estimates the trunk to have been 5.50m based on the still surviving remains.

An analysis of the DNA of the trees by Pankhurst (2014), suggests that Yew 1 and Yew 2 are clones. An unpublished dendrochronological report is mentioned by Pankhurst which dates Yew 1 at 1500 years. Unfortunately, this report was not available for inspection when requested.

An archaeological and desk based survey of the land holdings of the National Trust within the valley was conducted in 2007 by Oxford Archaeology North. The archaeological record for this valley is sparse compared with others within the Lake District (*e.g.* Quartermaine and Leech 2012). However, several other valleys are similar in having little or no settlement evidence during prehistory *e.g.* the Howgill

Fells (Bowden 1996), and Langdale (Edmonds 2004). Palaeoecological work at the nearby Johnny's Wood indicates there was no clearance prior to c.1200 AD (Birks 1993), though this was a small sampling site and may not reflect the wider valley. The lack of evidence for early settlement and clearance in Borrowdale may be contrasted with coastal areas, and what is now the moorland fringes where occupation was established in the Mesolithic and which, in some cases, were continuously occupied thereafter (Hodgkinson, et al. 2000, Loney and Hoaen 2006). Work by the author and other investigators on archaeological site survival in the uplands suggests that most of the suitable settlement sites where we might expect to find pre-medieval archaeology have been extensively reworked and so the low numbers of sites may be a reflection of later destruction (Hoaen and Loney 2006, Quatermaine and Leech 2012).

The archaeological record for the environs of the Yews is heavily dominated by sites relating to the adjacent graphite mines (Lax 1995), along with routeways, field boundaries and woodland exploitation (Scholfield 2007). Initial medieval settlement at the nearby Seathwaite Farm is thought to have begun prior to 1292 (Scholfield 2007), while work began at the local graphite mines sometime in the fourteenth century (Tyler 1995). At some point a trackway was constructed through the Yew grove and is recorded on the first edition of the Ordnance Survey map (OS 1860). Unlike other valleys a continuous ring garth was not established, which Scholfield speculates may be due to the high levels of rain. This, coupled with the tendency of streams to switch course, means that the traditional stone walls of the district are susceptible to undermining and subsequent collapse (2007).

In the present day, the Yews sit in an area of neglected wood pasture. In a review of the mapping evidence, it appears that the area between Yew Gill and New House Gill has been afforested to some degree since 1759. Scholfield speculates that *'there was never a period when the woodland had been clear felled between successive historic periods, allowing the continuity of woodland species. This has led to some species of relict pre-disturbance woodland (potentially pre-Norse) surviving in Borrowdale'* (op. cit.: 70). He then goes on to suggest that the Borrowdale Yews may be such a survival (Scholfield 2007).

Methodology

This was a 'slow' archaeological project, largely unfunded and taking place over several years. The site was first visited in the 1980s and it was recognised that the Yew trees were a significant element of the landscape, due to their great age and size and the possible presence of an earlier platform. Repeated visits demonstrated that the yews were located on an archaeological site, but other projects and interests prevented any attempt at formal measurement or description. The yews themselves were ancient and so formed a part of the cultural heritage of the valley. A site reconnaissance survey took place in 2013. Subsequently, several seasons of survey occurred and a GPS and offset survey of both the Yew trees and their environs were completed in 2016 together with a documentary search carried out at the Wordsworth Trust Archive.

Results

In a series of storms at the start of the 21st century, the trees suffered progressive crown loss, reminiscent of the hurricane of 1883 (Pankhurst 2014). As an attempt to protect the trees from grazing animals an enclosure was set up in 2005 (ibid.). This, together with the remains of the collapsed crowns of Yew 1 and Yew 2, has led to the site being overgrown by successional vegetation especially brambles and bracken, and makes surveying complicated as large parts of the site are obscured and hidden.

It is possible that the site is a small enclosure or platform more typical of the Scottish borders but also known from Cumbria at Deepdale (RCHME 1936). The outline of the possible platform is within the hachured area on Figure 3 where Yew 1 and Yew 3, are both associated with what appear to be archaeological features, some

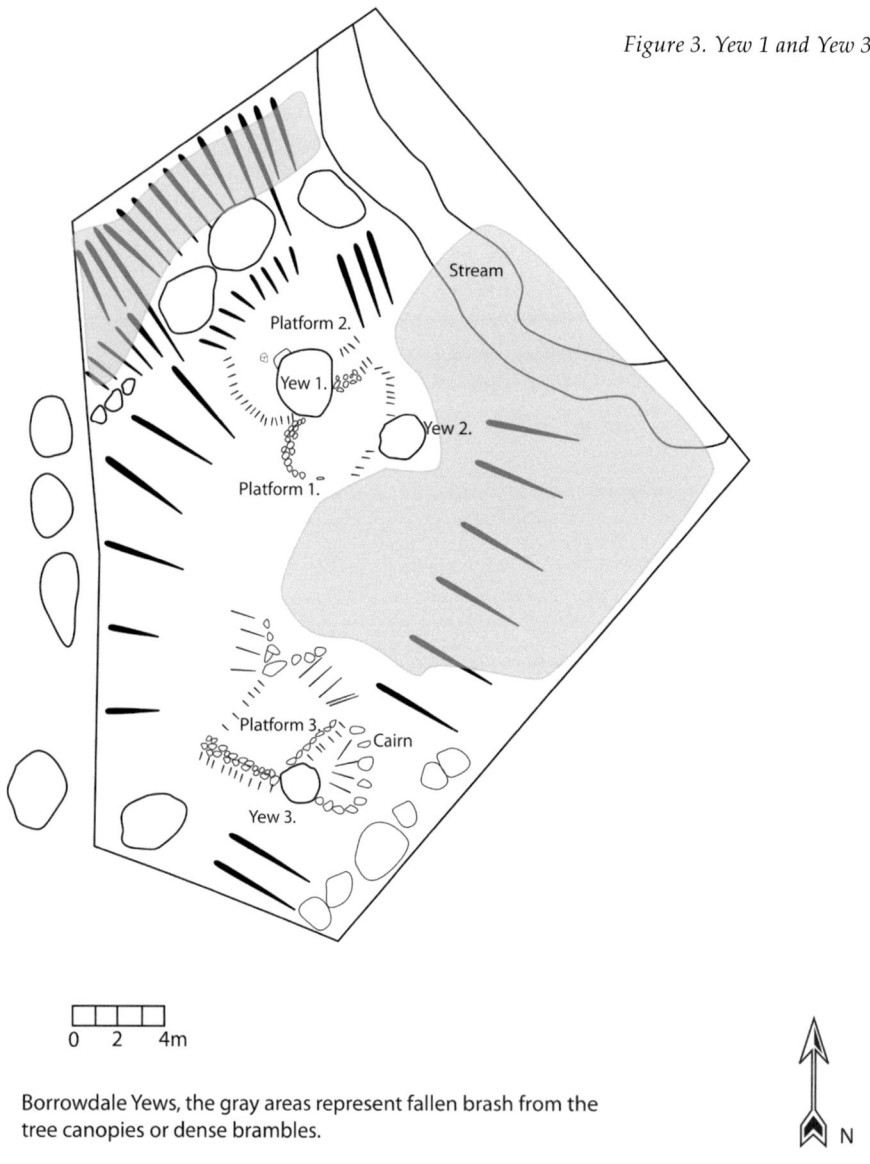

Figure 3. Yew 1 and Yew 3

Borrowdale Yews, the gray areas represent fallen brash from the tree canopies or dense brambles.

Figure 4. Graffiti from visitors on a boulder at the foot of Yew 1.

Figure 5. Detail of graffiti on a boulder at the foot of Yew 1.

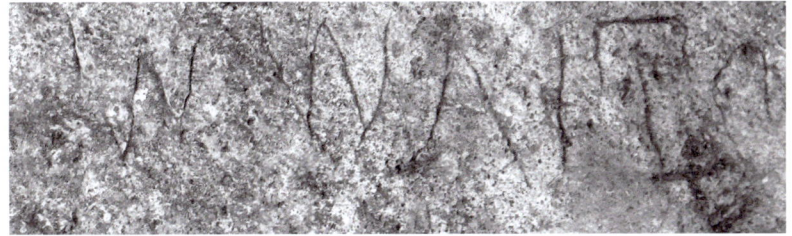

Figure 6. Detail of possible WW graffiti at foot of Yew 1. Possibly referring to William Wordsworth.

of which have developed after the growth of the Yews and some of which clearly predate them such as the platforms at Yew 1 and the cairn and platform at Yew 3.

Yew 1 is the oldest and largest of the trees, and has recently lost its crown for at least the second time in 130 years. Despite its great age, it is clearly a very resilient creature. There are two potential platforms (1 and 2) around this tree, a number of recent small stone constructions and firepits, and an earth grounded boulder with evidence of graffiti. The platforms appear to be overlain by the Yew and so pre-date it.

Platform 1 is located downslope of Yew 1, and is ovoid in shape (c. 6m x 3.5m) and is partly overlain by the trunk of this tree. There is a line of small boulders defining the edge of this platform which abuts the tree but it is not clear whether these are contemporary with the original platform or of later date. Downslope, the edge of the platform apron is defined by a low scarp.

Platform 2 is located upslope of Yew 1 and again appears to be overlain by it. This platform is circular and approximately 5m in diameter. On this platform are a number of recent hearths and attempts at building stone structures, possibly bivouacs or shelters. There is also a large flat stone embedded in the ground reminiscent of a cap stone. Partially overgrown by the tree is a large earthfast boulder with the carved initials, JP, JC, WW, and some that are illegible (Figure 4, 5, and 6). There are several hollows in the trunk which contain small stones (possibly placed there?), but there is no evidence of graffiti on the trunk.

Yew 3: upslope of this yew and slightly overlain by it, is a sub-rectangular platform c. 5m x 5m defined by scarps (c. 0.3m high) and low stone walls (c. 0.5-0.75m high). Downslope of the Yew tree is an ovoid cairn c. 3m x 4m defined by a kerb of low boulders. In winter when the vegetation is low it is possible to follow the line of the track, through the enclosure, which, as is customary in this district, is marked on either side by intermittent low boulders. Finally, the adjacent beck has shifted its course and now runs nearly adjacent to Yew 1.

The fellside adjacent to the yews is an area of what we might term exhausted pollards (Figure 7); these trees, mostly ash, are small, very rotten and neglected. The small size suggests that they may not be of great age, but trees in this type of marginal location are known to have very low rates of growth. There have recently been attempts to rejuvenate these pollards by trees surgeons (Pankhurst 2014; personal observation). Within this area of pollards are a small number of older mature trees including an oak, yew and ash with diameters ranging from 3.35m for the yew to 5m for the oak. The vegetation within this area, which is grazed by sheep, is now dominated by bracken which has expanded greatly since the foot and mouth outbreak of 2000 to 2001. The adjacent unenclosed Seatoller Woods forms part of the Borrowdale Woods Special Area of Conservation and is a SSSI because *"the lichen flora is known to be the finest of all woodland sites in northern England and the bryophyte species recorded from the wood are also outstanding"* (Natural England 1995). Despite the high grazing pressure in the recent past these woods have maintained a degree of botanical interest.

The survey within the area adjacent to the Yews conducted by the author was able to add a small number of sites to those located earlier, including three charcoal burning platforms and a pit (Schofield 2007). One of the charcoal burner platforms

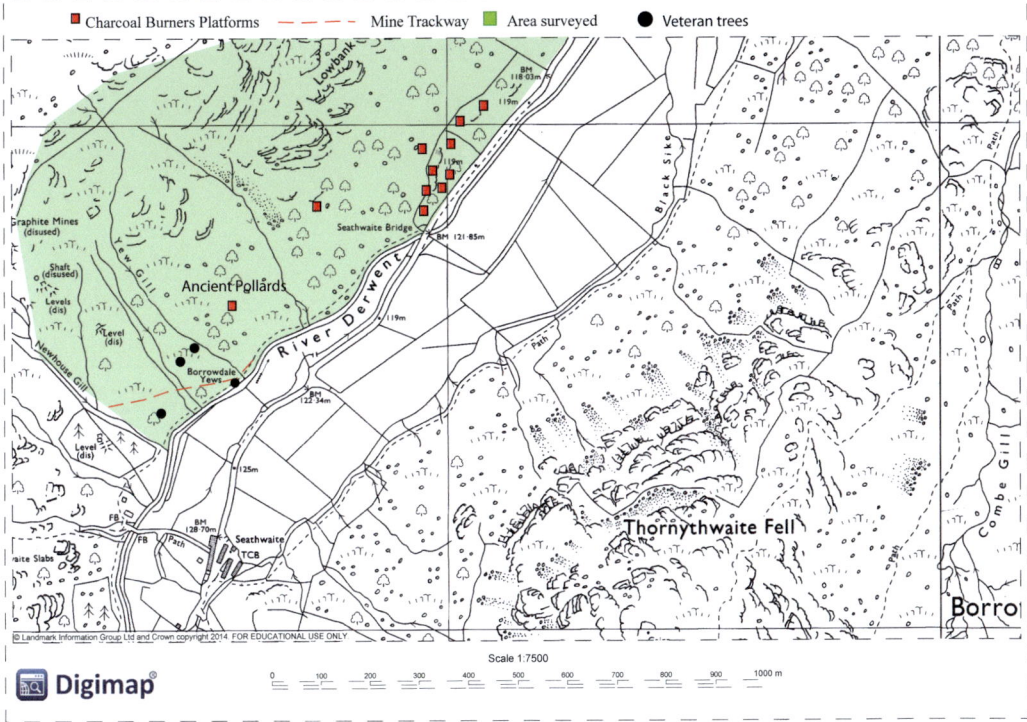

Figure 7.

underlies a later enclosure wall, which has been dated by the earlier survey to 1842 on the basis of cartographic evidence (Scholfield 2007).

Discussion

In the absence of excavation or any further palaeoecological work the following timeline of developments surrounding the Yews can only be tentative. At some point before the mid first millennium AD, one or possibly two platforms were constructed, possibly on a natural or artificially enhanced platform. Such platforms are known from elsewhere in Cumbria particularly on the eastern fells of the district (RCHME 1936, Quartermaine and Leech 2012). Excavations in Ullswater by the author have confirmed that small circular enclosures date to the Iron Age and were in use to the Roman period (Hoaen and Loney 2013). Excavations at Penrith Farm (Higham 1983) and Ribblesdale (Higham 1986) indicate that both curvilinear and rectangular forms were used in the Roman and immediate post Roman periods.

After the period of Roman occupation there was widespread abandonment of many sites (Higham 1986). If it is assumed that this site was also abandoned at some point in the first millennium AD, then the Yew grove forms part of the secondary woodland that developed within the valley. This would suggest that the Yew grove was already c. 500 – 700 years old when permanent settlement resumed in the early second millennium AD. The Yews thrived while generations of farmers, miners, woodsmen and other vibrant beings lived and worked in the valley. What use was made of the grove by the miners and the farmers in the valley we cannot know; there is no folklore associated with them, so all we know is that somehow, in this district, large yews were present and allowed to live, Yew trees are poisonous to livestock so consequently are not encouraged in areas dominated by pastoral farming, despite this being the main agricultural land use of the valley (Scholfield 2007). When Wordsworth visited in 1803 they were truly ancient, and part of a busy environment in which miners, shepherds and farm wives worked and which travellers from the north and south heading to the coast via Styhead Pass had to walk. There is not space for a full discussion of the graffiti here, but there is a possibility the WW may either be William Wordsworth himself, or a fan adding his initials to the place. This symbol may also represent the use of an earlier medieval piece of graffiti by nineteenth century tourists (Norfolk medieval graffiti survey (2020).

Fragments of the Wild: a conclusion

A traditional, anthropocentric archaeological account of the site at the Borrowdale Yews might mention the trees as a curiosity, but they would not be the focus. Indeed, if the trees had the misfortune to be just a little less old and a little less culturally important, it is likely that the local curators would have had them felled (on one of the sites I worked on in the Lake District, healthy mature ashes of 300 years were felled simply for growing on an archaeological site. They presented no threat but were untidy). Instead, the focus would have been on the platform remains and how they fit the chronology of the region, and affected our interpretations of the archaeology of the valley.

But the trees are there and they represent a significant survival of an earlier phase of the ecology within the valley. An anthropocentric view informed by the concept of the cultural landscape would take the perspective that these trees are not the result of a natural process, but rather the result of human interference first clearing the land, living in it, and then abandoning it.

If we draw on the ideas of Wordsworth, Snyder and Plumwood that nature and the wild are endlessly creative and active agents in their own right, then an ecocentric perspective would argue that this valley side is liminal, its environmental conditions are too extreme for permanent human settlement. It exists just beyond the bounds, but its stony soil, the high level of rainfall, the frequent and severe storms make it an impossible place for humans to settle and live permanently. It is worth remembering that although not a true mountainous area in the sense of the European Alps, it is still a dangerous place, and every year people are killed and injured in these hills; in 2014, the last year for which there are figures there were 9 fatalities, 237 injuries and a further 190 people had to be rescued on the fells of the English Lake District (Mountain Rescue 2015).

From an ecocentric perspective the valley side is a hybrid; dominated by an uncultivated flora it is wild and a wilderness, but at the same time it is also a place and a resource, integrated into the cultural, social and economic life of the mountain community. As Smout says in his essay on perspectives on landscapes in the North of Britain *"we live in nature and take delight from it"* (Smout 2000:7). Consequently, we should give equal agency to the wild plants and animals and processes that exist alongside, within and between the cultivated agency of the domestic plants and animals of the farm and field, when interpreting past and present environments. A perspective which mirrors that of Ingold (1993).

In such a reconstruction at times when anthropogenic factors such as grazing and woodland use are high, vegetation successions will develop that reflect anthropogenic pressure. The vegetation will tend toward open grassy pasture of poor quality, or that of a heavily managed woodland. When labour is short, or when grazing pressure or chemical use is low, extensive stands of bracken will expand to dominate the fellside as is the case in the present day. Eventually, if grazing pressure remains low, woodland will expand across the landscape to dominate and a true woodland ground flora will develop. This reversion to woodland has happened repeatedly in the past (Ratcliffe makes the point that images of Borrowdale from the 18th century show a deforested valley 2002:168).

Therefore, these ecological changes can be seen as the result of the wild agency of the plants and animals themselves. Rather than see these changes as the passive result of a relaxation of human management I suggest that we interpret them using the model of Snyder that new ecologies, new successions will develop upon abandonment. This is evident in a quote from the 13th century Trinity College Homilies: '[b]ut since they departed hence, the land lay useless, uninhabited and became waste, and it was completely covered in vegetation and so became wilderness' (in Jorgenson and Tylecote 2007:449).

In the case of the Borrowdale Yews, the opportunity arose for the colonisation and establishment of a stand of yews in the middle of what we might assume to be the type of wet oak forest that is characteristic of Borrowdale. This grove, once established became a fixture in the landscape, as although the woodlands that surrounded it have waxed and waned, the Yews have remained. They are just one 'fragment of the wild' in this valley, a part of a whole ecological palimpsest from the Ice Age survival of *Dryas octopetala* on the adjacent fell tops (Halliday 1997), to the Holocene oak woodlands of the Borrowdale Special Area of Conservation (Ratcliffe 2002). The plant assemblage that makes up the more intensively grazed parts of the area outside the bounds is itself formed of wild, not domesticated grasses and herbs, and is a hybrid succession evolved in part from the plants available at the original clearances.

Taking a contemporary archaeological perspective to environmental problems opens up the possibility for a new understanding of how environments and ecologies come into being and are sustained. This was a small study of a group of yew trees in an isolated valley in the north of England. Unlike previous archaeological investigations in the valley, the project experimented with using landscape archaeology techniques to study a group of 'living monuments' which earlier conventional landscape archaeology had overlooked. By careful mapping and analysis, it has been possible to demonstrate that the trees have grown over a pre-existing archaeological site, and that despite the use of the valley for pastoral agriculture and industry they have survived into the present day. As inspirations for Wordsworth's poem they have had a second existence as cultural and tourist heritage destinations which in turn has given rise to a series of graffiti and later shelters around the trees. As such these trees are embedded in the cultural and ecological present of the valley. As environmental archaeologists, we can make an important contribution to these vital debates around what is natural, and what is wild. These are important issues not just in archaeology but also in the present day contemporary world. Archaeologists have the methodological tools and long-term perspectives that allow us to approach these larger issues in the sciences and humanities, and the contemporary world is an excellent laboratory in which to study them.

Acknowledgements

Thanks are due to the University of Worcester who made equipment available for the surveys and funds for conference travel to present an earlier version of the paper. Thanks are due to the LAC conference committee for inviting me to speak and for the helpful comments. Thanks are due to the National Trust for permission to carry out the survey. Thanks are also due to the Wordsworth Trust for help with the archive search. Thanks are due to Helen Loney and Jennifer Peacock and two anonymous reviewers for comments on earlier drafts of this paper. The paper also benefitted greatly by reviews of Guillermo S. Reher and one anonymous reviewer.

References

Alexander, K., Allen, M., Butler, J., Green, T. & Woods, R. 2019. "Britain's natural landscapes- promoting improved understanding of the nature of the post-glacial vegetation of lowland Britain" *British Wildlife* 29(5): 330-338.

Barnes, G. & Williamson, T. 2011. *Ancient Trees in the Landscape: Norfolk's Arboreal Heritage*. Oxford: Oxbow Books.

Bate, J. 1991. *Romantic Ecology*. London: Routledge.

Bear, S. & Luther, C. 1998. "Indian Wisdom." In Callicott J. & Nelson, M. *The Great New Wilderness Debate*. Athens, Georgia: The University of Georgia Press, 154-198.

Bennett, J. 2009. *Vibrant matter: A political ecology of things*. Durham, North Carolina: Duke University Press.

Birks, H.J.B. 1993. "Quaternary palaeoecology and vegetation science – current contributions and possible future developments." *Review of Palaeobotany and Palynology* 79(1-2), 153-177.

Bowden, M. 1996. "Recent Archaeological Fieldwork in the Howgill Fells by the Royal Commission on the Historical Monuments of England." *Transactions of the Cumberland and Westmorland Antiquarian and Archaeological Society* Second Series 96, 1-12.

Buchli, V. & Lucas, G. (eds.) 2002a. *Archaeologies of the Contemporary Past*. London: Routledge.

Buchli, V. & Lucas, G. 2002b. "The Absent Present." In Buchli V. & Lucas, G. (eds.) *Archaeologies of the Contemporary Past*. London: Routledge, 3-17.

Callicott, J. & Nelson, M. (eds.) 1998. *The Great New Wilderness Debate*. Athens, Georgia: The University of Georgia Press.

Callicott, J. & Nelson, M. 1998a. "Introduction." In Callicott J. & Nelson, M. *The Great New Wilderness Debate*. Athens, Georgia: The University of Georgia Press, 1-22.

CBA. 2016. *Are Trees Archaeology?* (Online accessed 8/9/16) available at Are Trees Archaeology? – Young Archaeologists' Club

Coletta, W.J. 2001. "Wordsworth" In Palmer, J.A., Cooper, D.E. & Cooper, D. (eds.) *Fifty Key Thinkers on the Environment*. London: Routledge, 74-82.

Cummings, V. & Whittle, A. 2003. "Tombs with a view: landscape, monuments and trees." *Antiquity* 77(296), 255-266.

Curtis, J. (ed.) 1983. *The Cornell Wordsworth Poems in Two Volumes and Other Poems*, 1800-1807. Ithica, New York: Cornell University Press.

Dalglish, C. 2012. "Archaeology and Landscape Ethics." *World Archaeology* 44(3), 327-341.

Edwards, K.J., Fyfe, R.M., Hunt, C.O. & Schofield, J.E. 2015. "Moving forwards? Palynology and the Human Dimension." *Journal of Archaeological Science* 56: 117-132.

Edmonds, M.R. 2004. *The Langdales: Landscape and Prehistory in a Lakeland Valley*. Stroud: Tempus.

EU. 2016. *Wilderness in Europe* available at http://ec.europa.eu/environment/nature/natura2000/wilderness/index_en.htm accessed 12/02/17

Farley, F. & Roberts, M.S. 2012. *Edgelands: Journeys into England's true wilderness*. London: Vintage Press.

Fulford, T. 1995. "Wordsworth's 'Yew-Trees': Politics, Ecology, and Imagination." *Romanticism* 1(2), 272-288.

Fyfe, R.M. 2019. "Natural vegetation in Britain: the pollen-eye view." *British Wildlife* 29(5), 339-349.

Gaillard, M.J., Sugita, S., Bunting, M.J., Middleton, R., Broström, A., Caseldine, C., Giesecke, T., Hellman, S.E., Hicks, S., Hjelle, K. & Langdon, C. 2008. "The use of modelling and simulation approach in reconstructing past landscapes from fossil pollen data: a review and results from the POLLANDCAL network." *Vegetation History and Archaeobotany* 17(5), 419-443.

Garrard, G. 2004. *Ecocriticism*. Abingdon: Routledge.

Gilks, T. & Gilks, E. 1847. *Sylvan's Pictorial Handbook to the English Lakes*, re-published 1974. Dewsbury, Yorkshire: Evans and Longley Associates.

Graves-Brown, P., Harrison, R. & Piccini, A. (eds.) 2013a. *The Oxford Handbook of the Archaeology of the Contemporary World*. Oxford: OUP.

Graves-Brown, P., Harrison, R. & Piccini, A. 2013b. "Introduction" In Graves-Brown, P., Harrison, R. & Piccini, A. (eds.) *The Oxford Handbook of the Archaeology of the Contemporary World*. Oxford: OUP, 1-26.

Guha, R. 1998. "Radical American Environmentalism and Wilderness Preservation: A Third World Critique" In Callicott J. & Nelson, M. (eds.) *The Great New Wilderness Debate*. Athens, Georgia: The University of Georgia Press, 231-245.

Halliday, G. 1997. *A Flora of Cumbria*. CNWRS. Lancaster: University of Lancaster.

Hamilakis, Y. & A. Jones. 2017. "Archaeology and Assemblage." *Cambridge Archaeological Journal* 27(1). 77-84.

Handley, C. & Rotherham, I.D. (eds.) 2013. *Shadow woods and ghosts: A survey guide*. Sheffield: Wildtrack publishing.

Harrison, R. & Schofield J. 2009. "Archaeo-ethnography, Auto-archaeology: Introducing Archaeologies of the Contemporary Past." *Archaeologies* 5(2): 185-209.

Hay Festival. Rob Penn, Jill Butler & Justin Albert (speakers). 2015. Woodland Trust Series 1. The Country Living Debate: "Why Aren't Special Trees Valued Like Monuments?" Chaired by Kitty Corrigan. In association with Country Living magazine.

Higham, N.J. 1983. "The Excavations of Two Romano-British Farmsites in North Cumbria." *Brittania* 14: 45-72.

Higham, N. 1986. *The Northern Counties to AD 1000*. London: Longman.

Hindson, T. "The Borrowdale Yews." Taxus Baccata L. (unpublished) 2012. Available at http://www.ancient-yew.org/userfiles/file/Borrowdale1.pdf accessed 10/12/2016

Hoaen, A. 2019a. 'Wildness: Conceptualising the wild in contemporary environmental archaeology" *Internet Archaeology* 53. https://doi.org/10.11141/ia.53.3

Hoaen, A. 2019b.

"Environment and the senses" in *The Routledge handbook of Sensory Archaeology.* 164-178, Abingdon. Routledge.

Hoaen, A. & Loney, H. 2006. "The Precautionary Principle: Archaeological Site Recovery and Management in Light of Recent Work on Prehistoric Settlement in Upland Cumbria." *The International Journal of Biodiversity Science and Management* 2:150-154.

Hoaen, A. & Loney, H. 2013. "Landesque Capital and the development of the British uplands in later prehistory: investigating the accretion of cairns, cairnfields and ancient agricultural landscapes" In Gibson C. & Chadwick, A. (eds.) *Memory, Myth, Place and Long-term Landscape Inhabitation*. Celtic Studies Publications XVI. Koch, J.T. (ser. ed.). Oxford: Oxbow Books, 124-145.

Hodgkinson, D., Huckerby, E., Middleton, R. & Wells, C.E. 2000. *The Lowland Wetlands of Cumbria*. Lancaster: Lancaster Imprints 8.

Holtorf, C. 2013. "Material Animals: An Archaeology of Contemporary Zoo Experiences." In Graves-Brown, P., Harrison R. & Piccini, A. (eds.) *The Oxford Handbook of the Archaeology of the Contemporary World*. Oxford: OUP, 627-641.

Hoskins, W.G. 1969. *The Making of the English Landscape*. London: Hodder and Stoughton.

Ingold, T. 1993. "The Temporality of the Landscape," *World Archaeology* 25(2), 152-174.

Ingold, T. 2000. *The Perception of the Environment: Essays on Livelihood, Dwelling and Skill*. London: Routledge.

Jackson, K.H. 1971. *A Celtic Miscellany*. London: Penguin Books. 2nd edition.

Jorgenson, A. & Tylecote, M. 2007. "Ambivalent Landscapes-Wilderness in the Urban Interstices." *Journal of Landscape Research* 32(4), 443-462.

Latour, B. 2005. *Reassembling the Social: An Introduction to Actor-Network-Theory*. Oxford: Oxford University Press.

LDNPA. n.d. *Borrowdale and Bassenthwaite*. Available at http://www.lakedistrict.gov.uk/__data/assets/pdf_file/0009/729720/9.-Borrowdale-and-Bassenthwaite.pdf. Accessed 10/02/2017

Lax, A. 1995. *Seathwaite Graphite Mines Archaeological Survey Report*. RCHME (unpublished)

Le Guin, U.K. 1985. *Always Coming Home*. London: Gollancz.

Leopold, A. 1968. *A Sand County Almanac*. New York: Oxford University Press.

Lindop, G. 2015. *A Literary Guide to the Lake District*. Ammanford: Sigma Press.

Loney, H. & Hoaen, A. 2006. "Landscape, Memory, and Material Culture: Interpreting Diversity in the Iron Age." In *Proceedings of the Prehistoric Society* Vol. 71, 361-378.

Lorimer, J. 2015. *Wildlife in the Anthropocene*. Minneapolis: University of Minnesota Press.

Miller, D. 2010. *Stuff*. Cambridge: Polity.

Mills, C. 2013. *Hidden Heritage of a Landscape: Woodland Heritage & Dendrochronology at Arrochar* (unpublished report, Dendrochronicle) Available at: http://www.hiddenheritage.org.uk/docs/060_308__woodlandheritagedendroreportcmillsv2_1381137001.pdf Accessed 12/02/2017.

Mountain Rescue England and Wales. 2015. *Incident report 2014* Available at file:///Users/helenloney/Downloads/2014AnnualIncidentReportRelease21.pdf Accessed 12/02/2017.

Muir, J. 2008. *The Mountains of California*. London: Penguin.

Muir, R. 2006. *Ancient trees, living landscape*. Stroud. Tempus.

Naess, A. 1995. "The Deep Ecological Movement." In Sessions, G. (ed.) *Deep Ecology for the 21st Century*. Boston & London: Shambhala.

National Park Service. 1964. The Wilderness Act'. Available at https://wilderness.nps.gov/document/wildernessAct.pdf Accessed 10/02/2017.

Natural England. 1995. *SSSI listing for Seatoller wood*. Available at https://necmsi.esdm.co.uk/PDFsForWeb/Citation/1005549.pdf Acccessed 10/02/2017

Natural England. 1999. *Veteran Trees: A Guide to Good Management*. (online) http://publications.naturalengland.org.uk/publication/75035.

Norfolk medieval graffiti survey 2020 V V W and M symbols. Available at http://www.medieval-graffiti.co.uk/page15.html accessed 18/02/2020

O'Connor, T.P. & Evans, J.G. 2005. *Environmental Archaeology: Principles and Methods*. Stroud: Sutton Publishing Limited.

Oelschlaeger, M. 1991. *The Idea of Wilderness: From Prehistory to the Age of Ecology*. New Haven: Yale University Press.

Ordnance Survey. 2017. Digimap Roam. Accessed online at http://digimap.edina.ac.uk/roam/os 10/02/2017.

Oxford English Dictionary. 2017. Dictionary Available at http://www.oed.com/ Accessed 10/02/2107.

Pankhurst, M., A'Hara, S. & Cottrell, J. 2015. "The Fraternal Four." *British Wildlife*, 179-182.

Peterken, G.F. & Game, M. 1984. "Historical factors affecting the number and distribution of vascular plant species in the woodlands of central Lincolnshire." *The Journal of Ecology*, 155-182.

Peterken, G.F. 2019. "Defining natural woodland" *British Wildlife*: 30 (3), 157-159.

Plumwood, V. 1993. *Feminism and the Mastery of Nature*. London: Routledge.

Plumwood, V. 1998. "Wilderness Skepticism and Wilderness Dualism." In Callicott, J. & Nelson, M. (eds.) *The Great New Wilderness Debate*. Athens, Georgia: The University of Georgia Press, 652-691.

Plumwood, V. 2006. "The concept of a cultural landscape: nature, culture and agency in the land." *Ethics & the Environment* 11(2), 115-50.

POST. 2014. *Ancient woodlands* online Available at file:///Users/helenloney/Downloads/POST-PN-465.pdf Accessed 10/02/2017.

Quatermaine, J. & Leech, R.H. 2012. *Cairns, Fields, and Cultivation: Archaeological Landscapes of the Lake District Uplands*. Lancaster: Lancaster Imprints 12.

Rackham, O. 1990. *Trees and woodland in the British Landscape*. 2nd edition. London: J.M. Dent & Sons Ltd.

Ralston, I. 2004. "Archaeologists and the possibility of wilderness creation in Scotland," In Carver, E. & Lelong, O. (eds.) *Modern Views – Ancient Lands: New Work and Thought on Cultural Landscapes*. Oxford: British Archaeological Reports, British Series 377, 81-86.

Ratcliffe, D. 2002. *Lakeland: The Wildlife of Cumbria, The New Naturalist*. London: Harper Collins Publishers.

Rathje, W. 2002. "Integrated Archaeology: A Garbage Paradigm." In V. Buchli, V & Lucas, G. (eds.) *Archaeologies of the Contemporary Past*. London: Routledge, 63-76.

Rawnsley, H.D. 1884. "On the Yew Trees of Borrowdale," *Transactions of the Wordsworth Society* (no.6) p. 149-150 Available online at https://archive.org/stream/cu31924014138394/cu31924014138394_djvu.txt Accessed 10/02/2017.

RCHME. 1936. *Westmorland: An Inventory of the Ancient Monuments*. London: HMSO.

Richer, S. & B.R. Gearey. 2017. From Rackham to REVEALS. *Environmental Archaeology*. DOI 10.1080/141612103.2017.1283765.

Rotherham, I.D. 2011. "A landscape history approach to the assessment of ancient woodlands." *Woodlands: Ecology, Management and Conservation*: 161-184.

Scholfield, P. 2007. Borrowdale Cumbria. Historic Landscape Survey. (unpublished report) Available online at http://archaeologydataservice.ac.uk/archiveDS/archiveDownload?t=arch-815-1/dissemination/pdf/oxfordar2-28209_2.pdf.

Simms, S. 1992. Wilderness as a human landscape. In Zeveloff, V., Mcvaugh, W., & Zeveloff, S. (eds.) *Wilderness Tapestry: An Eclectic Approach to Preservation*. Reno: University of Nevada Press, 183-202.

Smout, T.C. 2000. *Nature Contested: Environmental History in Scotland and Northern England since 1600*. Edinburgh: Edinburgh University Press.

SNH. 2014. SNH's Mapping of Scotland's Wildness and Wild land: Non-technical description of the methodology (June 2014). Available at http://www.snh.gov.uk/docs/A1342460.pdf Accessed 10/02/2017.

Snyder, G. 2010. *The Practice of the Wild*. Berkeley: Counterpoint Press.

Soper, K. 1995. *What is Nature?: Culture, politics, and the Non-Human*. London: Wiley-Blackwell.

Spence, M. 1999. *Dispossessing Wilderness*. Oxford: Oxford University Press.

Thoreau, H.D. 2000. *Walden and Civil Disobedience*, edited by P. Lauter. Boston: New Riverside Editions, Houghton and Mifflin.

Tilley, C. 1994. *A Phenomenology of Landscape: Places, Paths, and Monuments*. Oxford: Berg.

Tyler, I. 1995. *Seathwaite Wad, and the Mines of the Borrowdale Valley*. Caldbeck: Blue Rock Publications.

Vera, F. 2000. *Grazing ecology and forest history*. Wallingford. CABI Publishing.

Vidal, J. 2003. "A bleak corner of Essex is being hailed as England's rainforest." Guardian Available online at https://www.theguardian.com/uk/2003/may/03/ruralaffairs.science Accessed 10/02/17.

Watkins, C. 2014. *Trees, Woods and Forests: A Social and Cultural History*. London: Reaktion Books.

Whatmore, S. & Hinchliffe, S. 2010. *Ecological landscapes in The Oxford handbook of material culture studies*, edited by D. Hicks and M.C. Beaudry. Oxford: OUP, 440-459.

Williams, R. 1973. *The country and the city*. London. Chatto and Windus.

Woods, M. 2001. "Wilderness: A Companion to Environmental Philosophy," In Jamieson, D. (ed.) *A Companion to Environmental Philosophy*. London: Blackwell Publishing, 349-361.

Wordsworth, W. & Bicknell, P. 1984. [1810]. *The illustrated Wordsworth's guide to the lakes*. London: Michael Joseph.

Geological and historical findings reveal differential anthropogenic substrate control in unique streets of Diemen, The Netherlands

*Ronald van Gelder[a], Sjoerd Kluiving[b],
Inger Leemans[b], Ruben den Ouden[c] & Jan Goedhart[d]*

a. Vrije Universiteit Amsterdam, The Netherlands
Contact-address: Schoolstraat 41, 1111 BP Diemen
b. 1. Faculty of Humanities, Vrije Universiteit Amsterdam, De Boelelaan 1105, room 14A-00, 1081 HV Amsterdam, Netherlands | 2. Research institute for the heritage and history of the Cultural Landscape and Urban Environment (CLUE+)
c. Municipality of Diemen, The Netherlands
d. Attis BV Consultancy, Dronten, The Netherlands

Introduction

Within the framework of a Ph.D. study in the field of 'Heritage Studies', we are currently carrying out research into the mutual influence of man and his natural habitat, in particular in the marshy west of the Netherlands. This research aims to contribute to the current discussion on the beginning, existence and definition of the youngest geological time scale: the 'Anthropocene' [1,2]. Currently the proposal to the International Stratigraphic Union is that the Anthropocene should have a lower temporal boundary dated to 1950 AD, coinciding with a suite of sharply increasing amount of anthropogenic materials, *e.g.* concrete, plastics, and most notably radionuclides[3]. The date of 1950 AD also coincides with what is known as the Great Acceleration [4,5]. Central to this paper are several basic questions, such as: can we clearly differentiate between natural and anthropogenic soil layers? What are the anthropogenic layers composed of? And to what extent can these human-induced layers possibly be differentiated in the soil?

---

1 C. Waters et al., "The Anthropocene is distinct from the Holocene". Science 351 (2016): 6269, at 137.
2 S.J. Kluiving, S.J. & A. Hamel. Human niche construction as a perspective on the Anthropocene. RCC Perspectives: Transformations in Environment and Society. Münich, Germany, 2016.
3 C. Waters et al., ibid.
4 W. Steffen et al., "The Anthropocene". Ambio 36 (2007): 614-621.
5 W. Steffen et al., "The trajectory of the Anthropocene". The Anthropocene Review 2-1 (2015): 81-98.

The present-day Dutch landscape has largely been formed in the last 150,000 years: the last two ice ages from the Pleistocene and Holocene, the current geological period. More than two-thirds of the Dutch surface is formed by Holocene deposits. The drowning history during the Holocene of various areas, such as the delta of the rivers Rhine and Maas, and such as the Wadden Sea and surroundings in the 'north', has been of great importance for the history of habitation in the Netherlands. Itinerant hunters and gatherers lived by hunting wild boar, red deer, otters, beaver, primeval cattle and moose.

Large peat areas were created behind the contiguous coastline of beach walls and low dunes: peat bogs on the west side, bog areas on the east side of the 'Netherlands'. The peat bogs fed on rainwater and therefore became constantly thicker. The hunter-gatherers made way for farming communities, which were being driven further and further to the east by the advancing peat. Initially, houses were built at ground level; but to protect themselves against flooding, people started to increase the living space. People created artificial residential mounds (terps).

The settlement has had a major influence on the current Dutch landscape with its dikes and polders, especially in the last 1000 years. Along the coast and rivers, dikes of natural material were constructed. In provinces such as Noord-Holland – wherein the village of Diemen is located -, large lakes were created by peat excavations – for peat extraction – and the first polders were constructed. In the latest centuries man built houses and all kinds of roads, creating villages and towns.

The human influence on the earth, on land for example, has even become so great that our (possible) successors can view our presence in the geological layers of the earth in thousands of years: in the (remnants of) sand extractions, canals, coal mines, apartment buildings, dams and shifted rivers. But, also through the natural and sustainable materials (such as glass and concrete, used in construction), and unnatural products, some of which are non-degradable (such as plastics, waste oils, waste products), with which we make the geological layers a serious and 'sustainable' threaten to pollute. This epoch with new layers of earth created by human hand is called the Anthropocene.

Research into anthropogenic earth layers is interesting because it can give us insight into modern time images and customs. For example, what materials and products people use in a certain region in a certain period, and how their choices change over time. Smith and Zeder (2013) articulate the goal of anthropogenic research as follows: 'A closer consideration of regional-scale documentation of the long and complex history of human interaction with the environment that stretches back to the origin of our species up to the present day' (Smith and Zeder 2013).

Much research in this subject-area hasn't been done yet, therefore previously conducted insightful studies are scarce. Kluiving, Van Gelder et al. (2017) executed a geo-archaeological pilot-study aiming to unveil the 'Biography of a house'. They studied the history of this 1930's house, among others by boring in the natural and cultural substrates the house was built on. And researched underneath the house, searching for traces of the first habitants of the place. The researchers were successful and able to retrieve old house-hold materials, products and clothes of the oldest inhabitants. These data in combination with historical and anthropological data collected are useful to unveil the 'Biography of the house'. Also, the aims of researches in the so-called *Garbage Archaeology* have much in common with the type of anthropogenic research in question.

If there is one type of soil in which the human influence on the natural environment can be observed, then it is the swampy soil in the western Netherlands, of which the peat was partly removed centuries ago. When houses are built or roads constructed on this soft soil, then care must be taken that they will not subside. The solution is not as simple as it seems. The soft, metres-thick remaining peat soil – which lies several metres below the surface, due to raising with all sorts of organic and inorganic remains by humans – settles under the weight of heavy constructions. This is why already from the 12th century AD, farms in this region were built on terps, which needed to be raised again every ten[6] to twenty years[7] because of the settling peat. Farm terps are an example of anthropogenic activity and a rich source of information on early humans and their impact on the surface of the earth[8,9]. For structures (such as stone houses and buildings) in Amsterdam, the capital of the Netherlands, which is located on the same swampy soil, wooden piles have been sunk into the ground since the eighteenth century[10]; the piles reach into the first (depth: 10-12 m. below National Ordnance Datum – N.O.D.) or second sand layer (depth: 25 m. below N.O.D.). The two deep layers of sand form a hard subsoil and were laid down during the last Ice Age, the Weichselian. The wooden piles under the centuries-old buildings are also a good example of an early human impact on nature. Sinking piles during construction – nowadays using concrete piles – as a matter of fact have always been and still is standard procedure in the western part of The Netherlands.

Streets and roads in the same region along the coast of the Netherlands also keep subsiding when nothing fundamental is done to prevent this. They constantly need to be maintained and raised, and it has been this way already for centuries.

The research is located in what was originally a farming village, Diemen, to the east of Amsterdam, located on the same soft soil as the capital. In Figure 1, the town and the village are central in the map, and the municipality of Diemen (in the past called 'Diemer bridge' (Diemerbrug), after the local bridge) is circled in red. What is clearly visible in this artfully created map is that town and village were located on a peat ('lilac-coloured') subsurface in 800 AD.

What the deeper layers of the eastern part of Amsterdam and the current village Diemen are constituted of, can be deduced from Figures 2a to 2c.

'De Nieuwe Buurt' is located directly on soft peat soil – the Formation Nieuwkoop Hollandveen (NIHO) (see Table 1). In contrast the Watergraafsmeer in Amsterdam-East is built directly on clay (Formation Naaldwijk/Laagpakket Wormer – NAWO). This is a consequence of the fact that Diemen is originally a peat polder and the Watergraafsmeer a marine clay polder from where the peat

---

6 W. Krook, "Opgegraven schoeisel uit de 12ᵉ eeuw". Tijdschrift Historische Kring Diemen 26-2 (2016): 46-48, at 46.
7 Blok (Ed.), Diemen in het land van Amstel.
8 Overbeke, van. Archeologische opgraving 'Boerderij Landzigt'.
9 J.A.G. Veerkamp, Terp-2; archeologische ontginningsterp Oud-Diemen. (Research master thesis Archeologie, Vrije Universiteit, Amsterdam 2011).
10 K. Koster, A geo-archaeological and historical geographical approach to examine 18ᵗʰ and 19ᵗʰ century pile driving in Amsterdam. (Research master thesis Geologie, Vrije Universiteit, Amsterdam 2011).

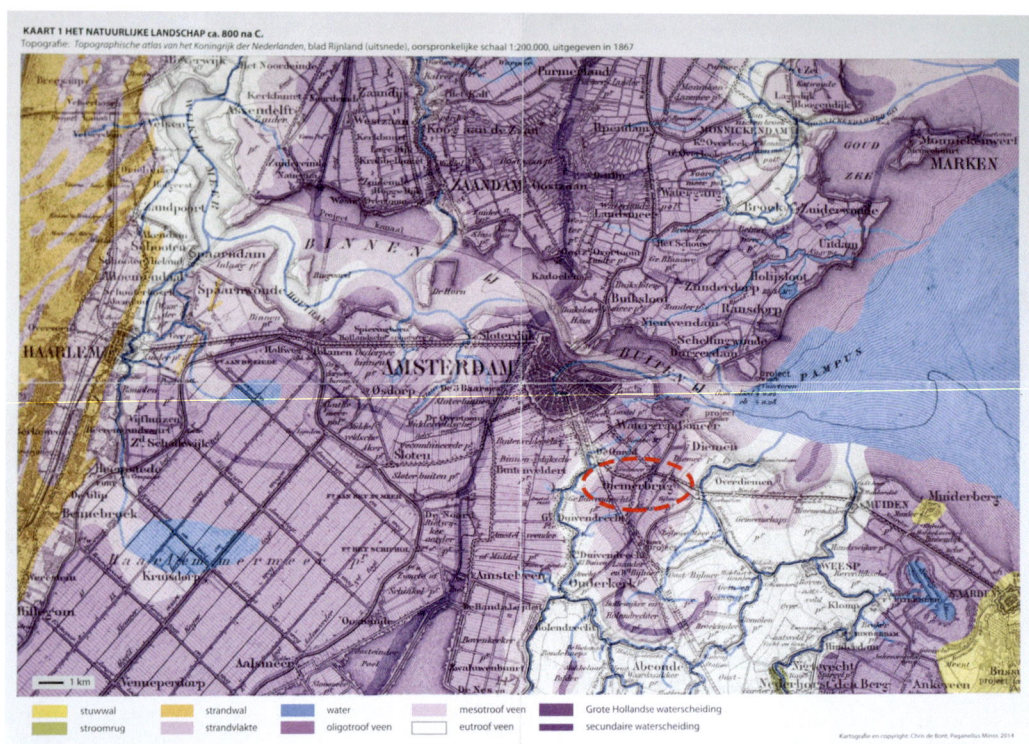

Figure 1. Projection of the ancient natural landscape in Amsterdam and its surroundings in ca AD 800 on the Topographische atlas van het Koningrijk der Nederlanden, page Rijnland (cutout), published in 1867. Cartography and Copyright: Chris de Bont, Pagamellus Minor, 2014. The capital of the Netherlands is located in the centre of the map, with the drained polder 'Watergraafsmeer' east of the town. Slightly further lies the village of Diemerbrug, which today is called Diemen. The capital and Diemerbrug lie on a soft soil of mesotrophic peat and clay.

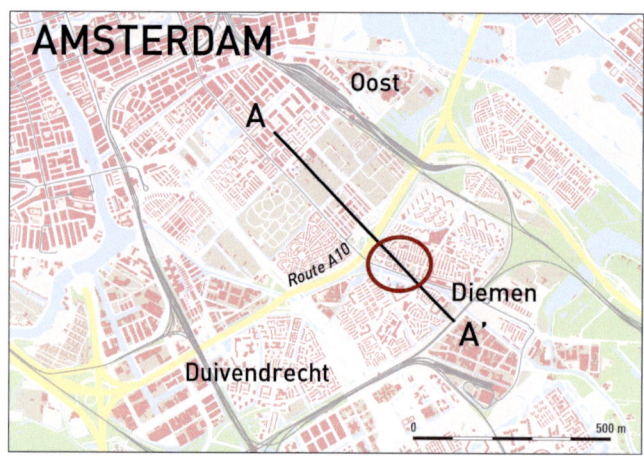

Figure 2a. Detail of the city map of Amsterdam-East and the adjacent municipality of Diemen. The line A-A' – from Amsterdam to Diemen – crosses the ring road around Amsterdam (Route A10 – in yellow). Just to the east of this ring road lies the municipality of Diemen; in the west of Diemen (Diemen centrum-west) is a neighbourhood, called 'De Nieuwe Buurt', wedged between the A10 and the local bridge over the barge canal. See Table I, Figures 2b and 2c.

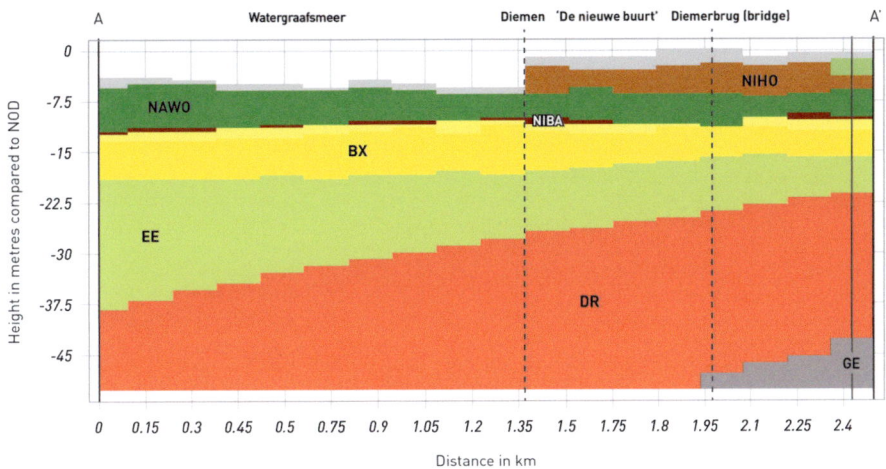

Figure 2b. Vertical cross-sections by means of GeoTOP v1.3 along the line A-A' (Amsterdam-East to Diemen). Just over halfway along the line, Diemen starts – in particular 'De Nieuwe Buurt'; just over three-quarters along the line A-A', Diemerbrug (bridge).
Legenda of colours: grey = anthropogenic deposits; orange = Nieuwkoop Formation/Hollandveen (peat); darkgreen = Naaldwijk Formation/Hollandveen (weak, half fluid clay); brown = Nieuwkoop Formation/Basisveen Bed (basic peat); yellow = Boxtel Formation (sand); light green = Eem Formation; pink = Drente Formation; turquoise = Ice-pushed deposits. For more information on the stratigraphic units see Table 1.

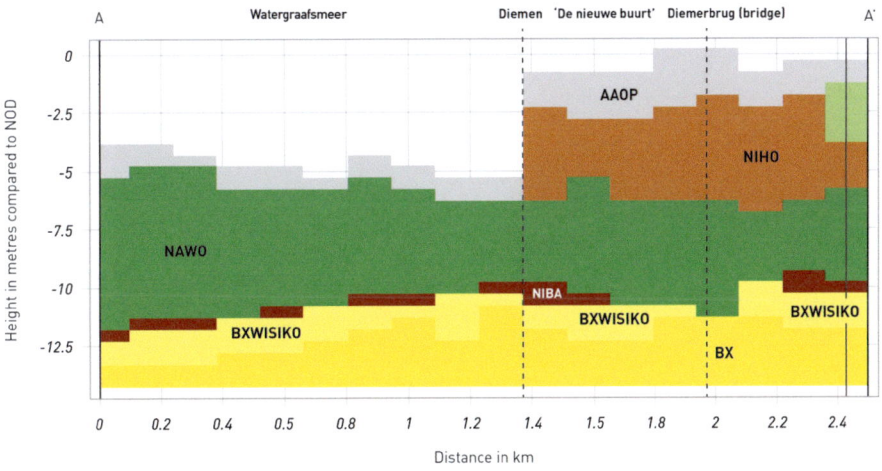

Figure 2c. This Figure is a detailed section of the vertical cross-sections of Figure 2b, to a maximum of 14 metres below N.O.D. The unique, metres-thick peat layer under a substantial anthropogenic soil layer in Diemen is clearly visible. A potential danger of that thick soil layer is that the peat settles at a higher rate when the weight on top is this great, or becomes even greater. Incidentally, it can be seen in this Figure how many metres higher Diemen (still) lies compared to the Watergraafsmeer, as a result of this peat layer.
Legenda of colours: grey = anthropogenic deposits; orange = Nieuwkoop Formation/Hollandveen (peat); darkgreen = Naaldwijk Formation/Hollandveen (weak, half fluid clay); brown = Nieuwkoop Formation/Basisveen Bed (basic peat); yellow = Boxtel Formation (sand). For more information on the stratigraphic units see Table 1.

UNIT GEOTOP	GEOLOGICAL UNIT	DOMINANT LITHOLOGY	DEPOSITIONAL ENVIRONMENT	AGE
AAOP	Anthropogenic deposits	Sand, medium fine to very coarse; clay, sandy, humic; domestic waste; construction material	Anthropogenic (made ground)	Late Holocene < 1000 years
NIHO	Nieuwkoop Formation, Hollandveen Member	Peat, sometimes clayey	Organogenic	Middle to Late Holocene 1000-5000 years
NAWO	Naaldwijk Formation, Wormer Member	Sand, very fine to medium coarse; shell-bearing; clay, sandy; sometimes humic	Marine (tidal channel and tidal flat deposits)	Middle Holocene 5000-8000 years
NIBA	Nieuwkoop Formation Basisveen Bed	Peat	Organogenic	Early to Middle Holocene 8000 years
BXWI	Boxtel Formation Wierden Member	Sand, medium fine	Aeolian (coversand deposits)	Late Pleistocene (Weichselian)
BX	Boxtel Formation	Sand, very fine to medium coarse; loam; clay, somtimes sandy, humic; peat	Aeolian, fluvial, lacustrine and organogenic	Late Pleistocene (Weichselian) 10.000-110.000 yrs.
EE	Eem Formation	Sand, very fine to medium coarse, shell-bearing; clay, sometimes sandy or shell-bearing; diatomite	Marine	Late Pleistocene (Eemian) 110.00-120.000 yrs.
DR	Drente Formation	Sand, very fine to very coarse, sometimes clayey; clay; sometimes sandy or varved	Glacial (meltwater deposits)	Middle Pleistocene (Saalian) 120.000-150.000 yrs.
GE	Ice-pushed deposits	Sand, medium fine to very coarse, sometimes gravelly; clay; sometimes sandy	Glacial (ice-pushed deposits of older formations)	Middle Pleistocene (Saalian) 150.000 years

Table 1. Lithostratigraphic units comprising the subsurface of Amsterdam and how these units are represented in the GeoTOP models (extracted from: J. Schokker, "3D subsurface modelling reveals the shallow geology of Amsterdam". Netherlands Journal of Geosciences 94 (2015): 399-417, at p. 401).

Figure 3. A view of the bridge of Diemen ('Gezigt van de Ringdijk na den Diemer brug'). The engraving by Daniël Stopendaal (1672-1726) from 1725 shows the Diemer bridge over the barge canal (previously named: 'Keulsche vaart'; nowadays: 'Weespertrekvaart'). Nearly three hundred years before the Amsterdam ring road (Route A10 – see Figure 2a) was constructed, horse riders rode on sand and tow paths in the same place (Overbeke, van. Archeologische opgraving 'Boerderij Landzigt', 11). Two hundred years after Stopendaal produced his engraving, 'De Nieuwe Buurt' was constructed to the left (to the north) of the barge canal – from the grove on the left in the picture to the Diemer bridge. (Collection Stadsarchief Amsterdam: drawings and prints).

has been reclaimed and removed since the last 400 years. Apart from that, the composition of the soil layers (see also Table 1) between Amsterdam-East and Diemerbrug is nearly identical to 45 metres below N.O.D.; the soil layers do, however, differ in their heights. See also Figure 2c.

The village of Diemerbrug was located on a barge canal constructed in the seventeenth century, between 1638 and 1640. On both sides of that canal were towpaths, so that the ships could be pulled along the canal. This can be seen on an eighteenth-century engraving of Diemerbrug (Figure 3).

The development of roads in the Netherlands has developed ever since. This was also the case for Diemerbrug, but road construction on a subsiding soil remained a major problem until the 1930s, even though it was in the twentieth century, after the industrial revolution, when the village of Diemerbrug slowly grew into the municipality of Diemen that we know today.

At that time, brick roads were built on manure, elder branches, fly ash and/or sand, to raise roads and prevent subsidence. For a short time, that was sufficient.

But the weight of such an extra body of soil, of the brick road and of the (at the time still limited) traffic soon led to such a degree of settling of the soft soil – on average about a centimetre per year[11] – that the council had to intervene after one or two years[12] and raise the ground again. Unevenness and bumpiness made the roads hard to use and thus unsafe.

The Archive of the municipality of Diemen contains more detailed geological information. The council claims: '… beneath the peat lies a layer of clay, but it is a very soft and wet clay with (probably) little more supporting power than the peat layer'[13]. And the Explanatory Memorandum of May 1935 states[14] that the roads in the western part of Diemen, adjacent to the Watergraafsmeer, were raised on average about 50 centimetres with black soil and again on average a metre and a half with sand. On top, bricks were laid to cover the road[15].

However, at the time the council was unsatisfied about the fact that the roads frequently subsided and that unsafe situations arose as a result of the constant settling of the soil[16]. Moreover, it felt that the financial costs for road maintenance became too high for the municipal budget. Both factors account for why the council tried out new foundation techniques[17,18] in this period, especially techniques supposed to be more sustainable and cheaper, which would thus lead to structural solutions.

---

11 Cf. Van Asselen, Peat compaction in deltas
12 Diemer Archives (1931-1987), INV. 85 Correspondence Council with Financial Department Haarlem, 6 april 1935.
13 Diemer Archives (1931-1987), INV. 85 Correspondence Council 6 oktober 1933.
14 Diemer Archives (1931-1987), INV. 85 Explanatory Memorandum B&W, 22 mei 1935.
15 Diemer Archives. Description on the backside of an undated and non-archived picture of the road. One of a series of pictures donated by the widow of the municipal building designer and clerk of the public works at that time, Jan de Boer.
16 Diemer Archives (1931-1987), INV. 85 Correspondence Council with Financial Department Haarlem, 6 april 1935.
17 It is highly probable that the municipality of Diemen was able to do groundcorings and measurements in 'De Nieuwe Buurt' with the aid of two independent Dutch institutes, working in the field: the Amsterdam 'Bureau Grondmechanica van Publieke Werken' and the advanced Delft 'Laboratorium voor Grondmechanica'.
18 Cf. Kuiper, Grondonderzoekingen en Betonberekeningen.

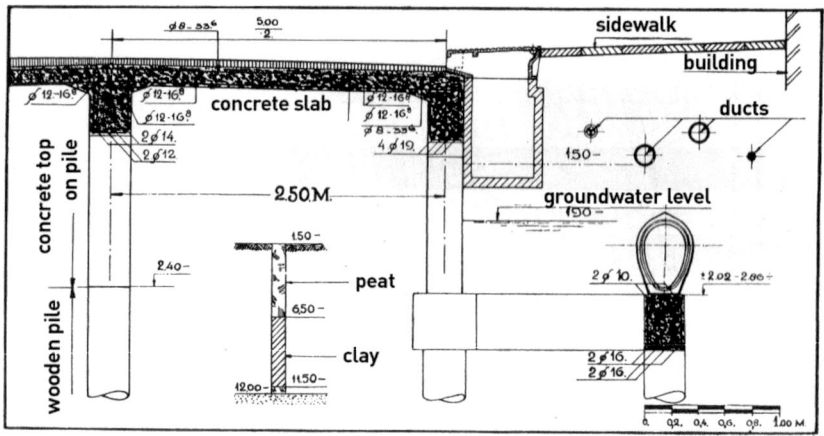

Road on piles (Diemen)

Figure 4. The roads were built on sunken piles according to Huizinga & Dibbits (T.K. Huizinga & H.A.M.C. Dibbits, De ondergrond der wegen. (Rapport, Association Internationale Permanente des Congrès de la Route, 's Gravenhage 1938). This is an original illustration from the report 'De ondergrond der wegen' (1938) by prof.dr. T.K. Huizinga (director laboratory for ground mechanics, Delft) and ir. H.A.M.C. Dibbits (engineer at Rijkswaterstaat). A whole page (pp. 30-31) of the report, which contained a series of lectures held at the VIIIth World Road Congress (1938) in The Hague (Netherlands), was devoted to the underground construction of 'De Nieuwe Buurt' in Diemen.

In the early 1930s, it was decided that hundreds of wooden piles with a length of 11-13 metres (reaching into the Late-Glacial sand of the Boxtel Formation) would be driven into the ground of 'Diemen centre-west', reaching below the ground water level (see Figure 4), for the building of a new neighbourhood between 1934 and 1936 (the so-called 'The Nieuwe Buurt')[19]. Concrete top-pieces were placed on top of the wooden piles, on which subsequently a road of reinforced concrete with an asphalt layer was laid (see also Figures 5a and 5b).

Clearly visible in this illustration is how the wooden piles sunk under the road are lengthened by concrete top-pieces. The tops of the piles are 50 centimetres below ground water level (- 2.40 N.O.D.).

The natural soil layers, depicted in the bottom centre of this 1938-illustration, roughly coincide with those recorded by the technical engineering agency MABEG, Utrecht and B.& W. Diemen (1935)[20] – cf. Figure 7-(coring)A and Table II-(coring) A. Only a few slight differences are visible when the records of MABEG et al. and those of Huizinga & Dibbits are compared; this mainly concerns the starting heights of the various soil layers.

---

19   Underpiling of a complete neighbourhood is unique. The Etruscs and Romans are said to be the first to underpile bridges and roads in their empires (Smolenaars, 2004). The Romans built 2000 years ago also roads on black oak-wood piles (Naber, 1999) in the 'Limes ad Germaniam inferiorem' – nowadays: The Netherlands, where the Dutch municipalities of Vleuten and De Meern are located. The idea of underpiling 'De Nieuwe Buurt' in Diemen stems – highly presumable – from the municipal building designer and clerk of the public works, Jan de Boer, who lived and worked in Diemen from 1929 to 1960.

20   Diemer Archives (1931-1987), INV. 85 Explanatory Memorandum B&W, 22 mei 1935.

Figure 5a. The Paulus Emtinckweg (one of the roads built on sunken piles) under construction in 'De Nieuwe Buurt'. In the background is the crossing Burgemeester Van Tienenweg (built on sunken piles in 1934), behind which the back of the Sint Petrus Banden church can be seen (1910); on the right of the photograph, parallel to the Emtinckweg, are the Schoolstraat (constructed in 1934) with the Sint Petrus school and on the other side of the road, houses. Visible sticking out above the houses is the roof of the former town hall of Diemen (1882). (Photography: Jan de Boer, 1934) For details on the location of the streets, see Figure 6.

Figure 5b. Under the road surface of the Schoolstraat. To the left, in the middle of the road, the concrete top-pieces on the wooden piles are clearly visible (Photography: Ronald van Gelder, 2013).

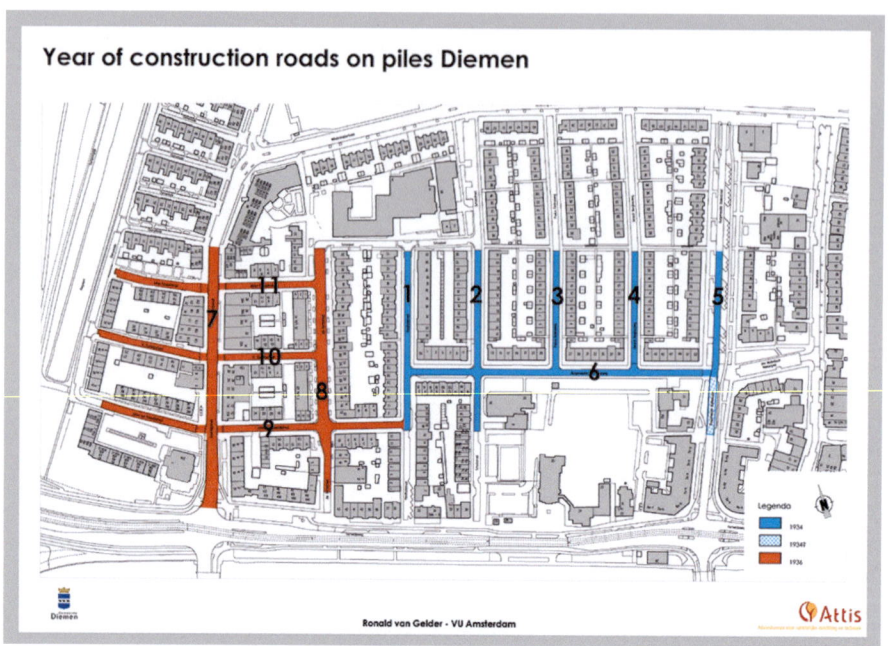

Figure 6. The neighbourhood was constructed by sinking piles in two phases; the 'oostwijk' in 1934 (blue) and the 'westwijk' in 1936 (orange) (Image design Attis BV Consultancy, Dronten The Netherlands). Streets and roads in the 'oostwijk (in blue)': 1. Raadhuisstraat, 2. Schoolstraat, 3. Paulus Emtinckweg, 4. Gerardt Burghoutweg, 5. Burgemeester Bickerstraat, 6. Burgemeester van Tienenweg. Streets and roads in the 'westwijk' (in orange): 7. Arent Krijtsstraat, 8. Jan Bertsstraat, 9. Johan van Soesdijkstraat, 10. Johan Coussetstraat, 11. Reinier Castelijnstraat.

The roads of the neighbourhood were constructed in two phases: piles for the eastern part of the neighbourhood (to be called: 'oostwijk' – eastern neighbourhood; Figure 6: street numbers 1-6) were sunk first in 1934 and subsequently for the western part of the neighbourhood (to be called: 'westwijk' – western neighbourhood; Figure 6: street numbers 7-11) in 1936.

To sum up, it is because of the constant interaction of humans and nature that the western Dutch soft soil seems eminently suitable for research questions related to soil characteristics concerning the 'Anthropocene' debate [21,22]. This is especially the case for Diemerbrug/Diemen, because the inhabitants of this region already had to resort to raising the subsiding natural soil with organic and/or inorganic materials at an early stage.

Second, the western Dutch soil is suitable to address Anthropocene research questions because the soil *under* the roads built on sunken piles seems easily accessible for further investigation.

---

21 C. Waters et al., "The Anthropocene is distinct from the Holocene". Science 351 (2016): 6269, at 137.
22 S.J. Kluiving, S.J. & A. Hamel. Human niche construction as a perspective on the Anthropocene. RCC Perspectives: Transformations in Environment and Society. Münich, Germany , 2016.

And finally – an additional factor – the local council workers, since the construction of the roads built on sunken piles in the 1930s, have accurately recorded and archived the state of the roads and what was done or should be done to them.

This unique combination of circumstances makes it possible to address the following research questions:

1. Which geological layers are to be found in the Diemen soil in the 20th-century 'De Nieuwe Buurt'? Do the layers of today (*e.g.* 2015) differ from the layers of several years ago (1935), when 'De Nieuwe Buurt' was built? Which soil layers are still the same and which are not?
2. What is the stratigraphical record of the shallow subsurface of Diemen, particularly in 'De Nieuwe Buurt'?
3a. Can different layers be distinguished within the anthropogenic soil layers in the separately investigated periods? If this is the case, how can these layers be characterised?
3b. Can the separately distinguishable anthropogenic layers be dated?
4. Is there a difference in penetration potential below the roads of the 'westwijk' and those of the 'oostwijk'? Can eventual differences be reduced to certain substrates and will it then be possible to date the emergence of these substrates?

Research methods

Archival research

The centuries-old, incompletely digitalised archive of the municipality of Diemen was and still is well maintained by the local archivists. Correspondence, reports of meetings, plans, drawings and designs related to the unique Diemen neighbourhood over time are relatively complete and documents are easily retrieved. In 2016, the easily accessible municipal archive was searched within the framework of our research and information relevant to the study was collected, analysed and used for the present article.

Technical inspections

Since the 1980s, five large technical inspections into the state of the roads built on sunken piles have been carried out, commissioned by the Diemen council (1986[23], 1994[24], 1996[25], 2013[26] and 2015[27]). The various technical inspection reports are also present and retrievable in the Diemen archive. Intensive use of the reports has

---

23 Haskoning, Onderzoek betonnen wegconstructies – Dienst gemeentewerken grondbedrijf Diemen (Technisch onderzoeksrapport, Haskoning Koninklijk Ingenieursbureau, Nijmegen 1986).
24 Haskoning, Onderzoek betonnen wegconstructies – gemeente Diemen (Technisch onderzoeksrapport, Haskoning Koninklijk Ingenieursbureau, Nijmegen 1994).
25 Omegam, Technische Inspectie van een wijk op palen in Diemen. (Technisch onderzoeksrapport, Onderzoeksdienst voor Milieu en Grondmechanica, Amsterdam 1996).
26 P. Hellinga, Bestaande betonnen wegconstructie te Diemen. Beschouwing. (Technisch onderzoeksrapport, Bartels, Leeuwarden 2013).
27 J.R.A. Kattenberg, Geotechnisch en milieutechnisch onderzoek. Wegreconstructie Centrum West Diemen. Plan van aanpak. (Technisch onderzoeksrapport, Mos Grondmechanica, Rhoon 2015).

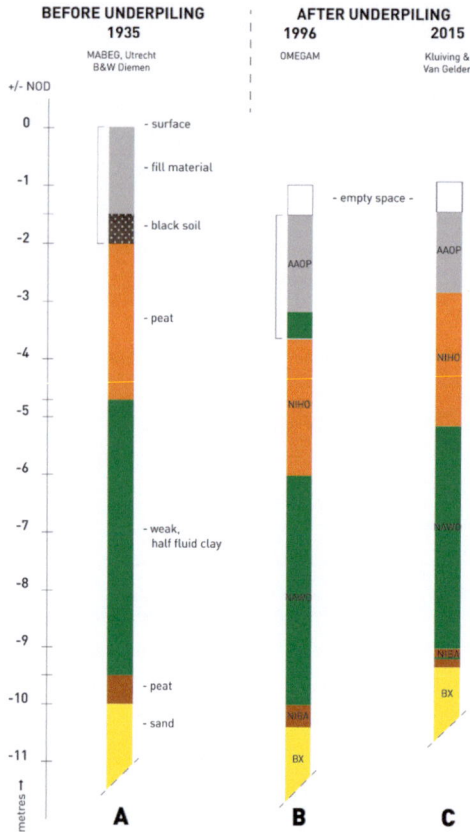

Figure 7. Comparison of corings in 'De Nieuwe Buurt', carried out in 1935 (A), 1996 (B) and 2015 (C). On the basis of hard circumstantial evidence, we are led to conclude that the municipality has inspected the underground in the area, denoted in this article as 'westwijk' (underpiled in 1936). For description of similarities and discrepancies between corings A, B and C, see results section: Table 2. Legenda of colours: grey = anthropogenic deposits; orange = Nieuwkoop Formation/Hollandveen (peat); darkgreen = Naaldwijk Formation/Hollandveen (weak, half fluid clay); brown = Nieuwkoop Formation/Basisveen Bed (basic peat); yellow = Boxtel Formation (sand). For more information on the stratigraphic units see Table 1.

been made in our study, especially the most recent technical report[26] which contains essential data for our research into geological soil layers. MOS carried out several depth probes and extensive corings under the various roads of the neighbourhood. Aggregation of data relevant to us, plus recalculation and reanalysis of the various results provided important information for our study.

Hand corings

The first two authors of the present paper have carried out test corings with a hand core in representative roads of the Diemen neighbourhood. These corings were carried out in the Gerardt Burghoutweg (in the 'Oostwijk', piles sunk in 1934; Figure 6, street number 3) and in the Jan Bertsstraat (in the 'Westwijk', piles sunk in 1936; Figure 6, street number 8). A hand core (Edelman, 7 cm width) with several long T-parts and a gauge core of 90 centimetres (3 cm width) long were used. Hand corings were carried out to a maximum depth of 10 metres.

Results

Two technical reports from the archives of the municipality of Diemen (from 1935 and 1996), and an internal publication from VU University Amsterdam (2015)[28], about recently executed coring research present the results of three representative geological corings in study area of 'De Nieuwe Buurt' (Figure 7). The earliest coring from 1935 was executed by the technical company MABEG from Utrecht, hired by the late Council of Diemen in the 1930s (Figure 7-(coring)A); the latest coring (2015) was done by Kluiving & Van Gelder (Figure 7-(coring)C), and the coring in between was carried out by the Amsterdam Research Agency for Environment and Ground Mechanics (Onderzoeksdienst voor Milieu en Grondmechanica – OMEGAM) in 1996 – Figure 7-(coring)B.

A comparison of the three cores show between -9 and -11 meters below ordnance datum the top boundary of a sand unit (BX, Figure 7). That has been interpreted as the Boxtel Formation, dating from the last Glacial. All three cores show a thin unit (0,5 – 0,2 m) of peat, Basal Peat (NIBA), occurring on top of the sand. The basal peat reflects the influence of rising groundwater as a consequence of rising sea level in the Early Holocene, between 7,000 and 9,000 years ago.[29] A 3 -5 thick meter clay unit, also described as a 'weak, half-fluid clay' with shell fragments has been interpreted as the Wormer Member of the Naaldwijk Formation (NAWO) and follows the basal peat concordantly on top of it (see Figure 7). The transition from the clay to reed peat and sedge peat marks the closing of the Holland tidal basin with sand bars further west. As a consequence of the decreased energy conditions and transition between an open and closed coast in the Holocene history of the western Netherlands, the peat developed as a 2-3 thick meter peat layer and is interpreted as the Hollandveen layer of the Nieuwkoop Formation (NIHO).

On top of the Hollandveen layer the unit between the three cores slightly varies (see Figure 7): core A has a 'black soil' followed by fill material until the surface, core B shows a clay layer with little debris followed by a weak silty sand with little too much debris interpreted as an 'anthropogenic layer', similarly as in core C the anthropogenic layer (AAOP). As defined earlier, an anthropogenic layer is regarded as a geological layer in which the mutual influence of humans and their natural habitat is clearly notable.

The anthropogenic layers in the Diemen soil, at the location of 'De Nieuwe Buurt', can clearly be distinguished from the natural soil layers. Within these anthropogenic soil layers, several different layers can be distinguished in the separately investigated periods: in 1935 (Figures 7-(coring)A and Table 2-(coring) A), there is a layer of black soil in the 'westwijk' with a layer of material on top to raise the ground (the grey block in the Figure). The raised layer contains fly ash

---

28 S.J. Kluiving and R.S. van Gelder, Geological investigation of the Gerardt Burghoutweg in Diemen (The Netherlands) (Internal publication, Vrije Universiteit, Amsterdam 2015).
29 J. Schokker et al., "3D subsurface modelling". Netherlands Journal of Geosciences 94 (2015): 399-417, at 401.

and sand, according to the then leading municipal building designer De Boer[30]. In the anthropogenic layer (Figure 7-(coring)B/Table 2-(coring)B) mentioned in the inspection report from 1996, clayish sand and peat (the green block) and 'redeposited soil and rubble'[31] was found in the 'westwijk' – grey block in Figure 7-B. The anthropogenic layer observed in 2015 (Table 2-(coring)C – in the 'oostwijk') contained mainly sand as a raising material (grey block in Figure 7-C).

Most of the lithostratigraphy in the Diemen soil, at the location of 'De Nieuwe Buurt', has stayed the same in the past century with regard to the soil layers found today in corings, but the layer contacts are not identical in elevation everywhere. The layer contacts of the soft peat and clay layers (NAWO and NIHO) from 1935 (Figure 7-A), vary considerably up to meter 1.5, especially the upper contact of the NIHO layer, during the century (Figures 7-B and 7-C).

The anthropogenic soil layer has changed strongly over time (Figure 7a-A-B-C). The raised layers observed in 1935 (Figure 7a-A) are suggested to have been laid down in 1929 during the original construction of the roads of the 'westwijk' – before the underpiling. The raised material in the 'westwijk' found in the technical report from 1996 dates from the time that the underpiled roads were constructed in 1936. The raised material found in 2015 in the 'oostwijk' dates from 1934 and from later – limited – extra deposits of sand, necessary to prevent movement and sliding of 'dune or river sand' from under the pavements to the empty spaces under the road (Personal Messages, Kooijman resp. Berkhout, 2015)[32].

During the fieldwork there appeared to be a difference in corability between the hollow spaces under the roads in the 'westwijk' and those in the 'oostwijk'. Reanalysis and recalculation of the data from the technical research report of Technisch Bureau MOS Grondmechanica from Rhoon[33] led to the conclusion that materials of a completely different consistency lay under the surface of the roads of the 'westwijk' (underpiled in 1936) and those of the 'oostwijk' (underpiled in 1934). Under the roads of 1934 ('oostwijk') there is a clear distinction between the natural soil layers consisting of weak silty peat or mineral-poor peat (Dutch: rietzeggeveen) and culturally deposited layers consisting of weak silty sand or silty peat around the means of 3.9 m. and 3.2 m. below NOD. Under the roads constructed in 1936 ('westwijk') this distinction is completely absent – anthropogenic layers make it impossible to core through the ground surface, which consists – at about a mean of 2.45 m. below NOD – of weak silty sand, with slickstones and punestones added.

---

30 Diemer Archives. Description on the back of an undated and non-archived picture of the road. One of a series of pictures donated by the widow of the municipal building designer and clerk of the works at that time, Jan de Boer.
31 Diemer Archives INV. 5733: Bestek van gemeentelijke Dienst, 1935.
32 Personal messages from former labourers of Diemen public works: Hans Kooijman (Lelystad, The Netherlands) resp. Rob Berkhout (Almere, The Netherlands), 26 april 2016.
33 J.R.A. Kattenberg, Geotechnisch en milieutechnisch onderzoek. Wegreconstructie Centrum West Diemen. Plan van aanpak. (Technisch onderzoeksrapport, MOS Grondmechanica, Rhoon 2015).

A		B		C	
BEFORE UNDERPILING		**AFTER UNDERPILING**		**AFTER UNDERPILING**	
YEAR OF RESEARCH	1935	YEAR OF RESEARCH	1996	YEAR OF RESEARCH	2015
SURFACE	50 cm. above NOD	SURFACE	83 cm. below NOD	SURFACE	80 cm. below NOD
GEOLOGICAL UNITS		GEOLOGICAL UNITS		GEOLOGICAL UNITS	
UNIT GeoTOP		UNIT GeoTOP		UNIT GeoTOP	
AAOP	heightening added: black soil	AAOP	empty space	AAOP	empty space
	0 - 1,50m. below NOD		*fill material*		*fill material:*
	1,50 m. - 2,00 m.		sand (moderate fine), weak silty, with little debris		clayey, silty sand
			80 cm. - 1,40 m.		80 cm. - 1,50 m.
			sand (moderate fine), weak silty, with much debris		
			1,40 m. - 3,1 m.		1,50 m. - 3,00 m.
			clay (solid), weak silty, weak soily, with little debris		
			3,1 m. - 3,5 m.		
NIHO	peat	NIHO	peat (solid)	NIHO	Hollandveenpackage
	2,00 m. - 4,7 m.		*locally formed material:*		sedge peat
			Hollandpeat		reed peat
			3,5 m. - 5,9 m.		3,00 m. - 5,00 m.
NAWO	weak, half fluid clay	NAWO	clay (moderate weak, moderate solid and solid)	NAWO	blue clay
	4,7 m. - 9,5 m.		wad deposition		Wormerlaagpackage
			5,9 m. - 9,9 m.		5,00 m. - 9,50 m.
NIBA	peat	NIBA	peat (solid), weak clayey	NIBA	basal peat
	9,5 m. - 10,00 m.		*locally formed material:*		brown and blue clay
			basal peat		basal peat
			9,9 m. - 10,3 m.		9,00 m.
					9,05 m.
					9,30 m.
BX	sand	BX	sand (very fine) weak silty, weak soily	BX	sandlayer of last Ice Age
	10.00 m. and deeper		periglacial deposition		top of Pleistocene
			10,3 m. and deeper		9,40 m. and deeper
RESEARCHERS	MABEG, Utrecht	RESEARCHERS	OMEGAM, Onderzoeksdienst voor Milieu en Grondmechanica, Amsterdam	RESEARCHERS	Kluiving S.J. & Van Gelder R.S., VU University Amsterdam
REFERENCE	*Explanatory Memorandum of The Mayor and City Counsel Members Diemen, May 22 1935. (in: Archives of Municipality Diemen)*	REFERENCE	*Report of Technical Inspection Underpiled roads of Diemen Amsterdam, May 13 1996. (in: Archives of Municipality Diemen)*	REFERENCE	*Gelder, R.S. van, Kluiving, S.J. Leemans, I.B.Ouden, R. den & Goedhart, J. Geological findings in unique streets of Diemen, The Netherlands, reveal different anthropogenic substrate control Presentation at 4th International Landscape Archaeology Conference. Uppsala: 22-25 August 2015.*
LOCATION	western part of neighbourhood (no further specifications)	LOCATION	western part: Arent Krijtsstraat (see figure 6, street number 7)	LOCATION	eastern part: Gerardt Burghoutweg (see figure 6, street number 4)

Table 2: Detailed information about the three respective cores A, B and C, and reports mentioned above. Table 2-A relates to Figure 7-A, Table 2-B relates to Figure 7-B and finally, Table 2-C to Figure 7-C. For further explanation with regard to the geological soil layers mentioned here, see Table 1.

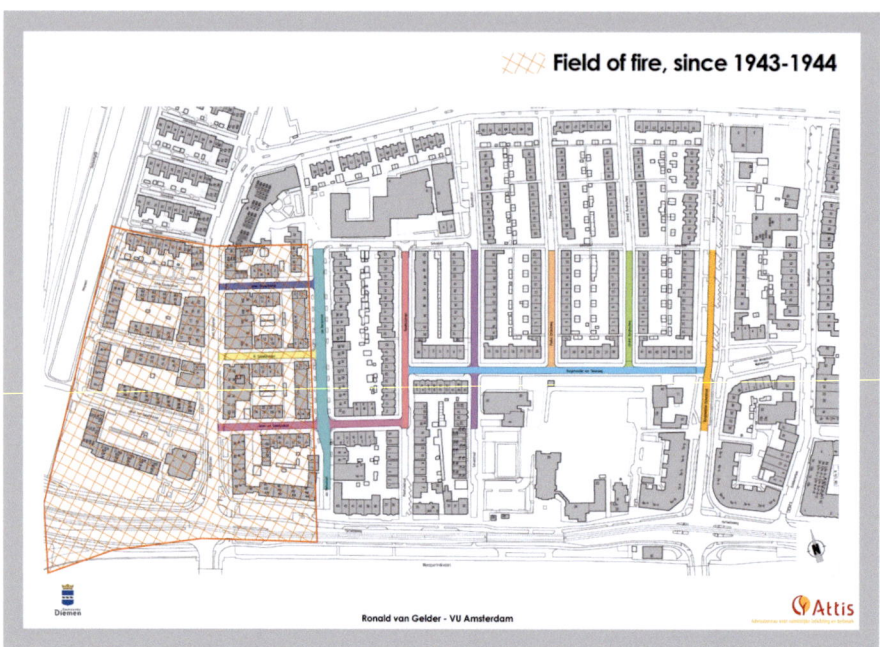

Figure 8a. During World War II the German occupier tore down one third of the neighbourhood on piles, namely the western part. The area, according to the Germans was urgently needed as a field of fire to defend Amsterdam against their enemies. The western part of the neighborhood (on the left) is marked in the illustration by hatching. Image design by Attis BV Consultancy, Dronten The Netherlands.

Figure 8b. The western part of the neighbourhood is completely demolished. The eastern part is untouched, which is visible in the background of the picture. Photography: A. Magrijn-Hooiveld (1943).

Discussion

Contrast in anthropogenic layers of 'westwijk' and 'oostwijk'

Ground corings by hand by Kluiving & Van Gelder (2015) yielded identical research results. The sunken-pile construction under the Jan Bertsstraat (representative for the 'westwijk') is *not* corable below -2.50 N.O.D. due to the presence of stones, little and heavy debris and rubble, whereas the road constructed on sunken piles of the Gerardt Burghoutweg representative for the 'oostwijk' is. The geological layering of this latter road can be mapped easily, even to a great depth (a minimum of 10 metres below N.O.D.). It is not immediately clear why and since when the substrate of the 'westwijk' has been difficult to penetrate.

How can it be explained that the roads of the 'oostwijk' (underpiled in 1934) turn out to be easily penetrated while the roads of the 'westwijk' (underpiled in 1936) are not? The first explanation is that the streets under the 'westwijk' were already constructed in 1929 on a foundation of black soil and raised materials, such as fly ash and sand. Until 1936, these streets were raised with cheap residual materials, so probably also with fine and course rubble, to maintain the elevation of the road surface. The underpiled road was constructed on top – on wooden piles – in 1936. There was no empty space under the road – that is why the top layer of these roads is not easy to core. An explanation why this is different for the roads of the 'oostwijk' is probably due to the fact that these roads were constructed high above a wasteland that had not been raised.

A second explanation is related to the economic circumstances in 1934, which were better compared to those in 1936 (in the middle of the crisis years); that is why it was easier to financially complete projects in 1934 than in 1936. For example, the government contributed to a greater extent to the payment – and thus motivation – of roadworkers in 1934, for instance through employment projects for the unemployed. And – as was also discovered during recent technical research under the roads[34] – , of the materials used in 1934 (such as wooden piles, but also the raw materials necessary for road construction) were of a higher quality and were used to a greater degree compared to the road building in 1936. The quality control of the construction in 1934 was also much better than in 1936. Overall, as a result the roads in the 'westwijk' are considerably less sustainable than those in the 'oostwijk'.

Another alternative explanation for the observed difference is related to the demolition of the 'westwijk' by the Germans during the Second World War to create a field of fire and to protect Amsterdam from enemy aerial attacks. This part of the neighbourhood was demolished to the ground by the German occupiers in late 1943, early 1944 – see Figures 8a and 8b. At that time, the houses and buildings were systematically broken down – 32% of the housing stock in Diemen – and the remaining usable materials were transported to Germany by ship. The ships left along the Weespertrekvaart (see also Figure 3) – the former Keulsche Vaart – to war-stricken areas in Germany, such as Cologne[35] and Hamburg. As a matter of

---

34   Personal message: Jan Goedhart (2015), Attis BV Consultancy, Dronten, The Netherlands.
35   Literally is 'the Keulsche Vaart': the barge canal to Cologne in Germany.

fact the text 'Liebesgaben aus den Niederlande' was written on the ships' hulls! The inhabitants of the 'westwijk' had to move to a neighbourhood in *Amsterdam*, the Jewish inhabitants of which had been deported by the Germans. The demolition was contracted out by the Germans to collaborating Dutch companies, which carried out the demolition of the neighbourhood and the loading of the ships for them for a paltry fee. It is not unthinkable that the underpaid employees of these companies were not very particular about the – poorly paid, but urgent – commission and that they dumped scrap material under the underpiled roads.

A final explanation is a combination of the second and third explanations. It is possible that the already less durable roads in the 'westwijk' deteriorated more due to the demolition of houses and buildings, the clearing of rubble and preparation for the construction of the field of fire than the roads in the 'oostwijk', where this dramatic scenario never took place.

The historical developments in the research area Nieuwe Buurt are potentially correlated to the described stratigraphy of the anthropogenic deposits. This paper provides the first step in order to collect more combined historical and geological data to support the so-called 'late' hypotheses of the onset of the 'Anthropocene'[36]. Is the process of improving road conditions in the 1930s a consequential developmental step after the Industrial Revolution and an unavoidable preamble for the Great Transformation[37,38]?

Conclusion

Archival and literature studies (Diemer Archives: 1986, 1996, 2000, 2015) as well as our own cores have demonstrated that the soil under the Diemen neighbourhood 'De Nieuwe Buurt' has consisted of the same soil layers (lithostratigraphy) for nearly a century[39]. Under the anthropogenic first soil layer, the natural soil layers of, in succession, peat, clay, basal peat and a sturdy layer of sand, a remnant of the last Ice Age, are found. The elevations of the layer contacts of the natural strata, however, appear to have changed a little over time: in particular the highest peat and clay layers have subsided – almost certainly also[40] due to settling over the last 80 years.

The top, anthropogenic soil layer has certainly changed during the course of the century; this appears not only from the archival and literature studies concerned, but just as much from the cores we carried out ourselves in this soil layer in the Diemen neighbourhood. These deviations can mainly be found in a part of Diemen centre-west, the so-called 'westwijk', which was underpiled in 1936. The anthropogenic layer from before 1936 turns out to consist of black soil and raised material: 'redeposited soil and sand', as the plans at the time mention[41]. Later, investigations in this location mainly encountered fly ash and sand with fine or coarse rubble in this first soil layer(s) (1996). The research report of MOS

---

36 C. Waters et al., "The Anthropocene is distinct from the Holocene". Science 351 (2016): 6269, at 137.
37 W. Steffen et al., "The Anthropocene". Ambio 36 (2007): 614-621.
38 W. Steffen et al., "The trajectory of the Anthropocene". The Anthropocene Review 2-1 (2015): 81-98.
39 The focus is mainly directed here at the first 10-12 metres below N.O.D. – untill the first sand layer.
40 According to calculations, the western parts of Holland have lowered in the past 1000 years for more than three metres.
41 Diemer Archives INV. 5733: Bestek van gemeentelijke Dienst, 1935.

Grondmechanica[42] and our own corings even show that we cannot core through these first soil layers under the underpiled roads in the 'westwijk' to a depth of more than 2.5 metres below N.O.D. A remarkable finding. And this while the council of Diemen at that time so clearly stated in its plans for underpiling of the roads that: 'eventually hollow spaces will arise under the roads and under the beams on which the sewers are laid'[43].

The most likely explanation for this is that the streets under the 'westwijk' were already constructed in 1929 on a foundation of black soil and raised materials, such as fly ash and sand. Up to 1936, these streets were raised with cheap residual materials, including fine and course rubble, to maintain the height of the road surface. And in 1936 the underpiled road – on wooden piles – was constructed on top. No space remained under the road – that is why the top layer of these roads is not easily corable; at least in the locations where the most recent studies were carried out (by MOS Grondmechanica in 1996 and Kluiving & Van Gelder in 2015). That this is different for the roads of the 'oostwijk' is related to the fact that these roads were constructed high above a wasteland that has never been raised. Further research will reveal whether these are the correct hypotheses.

Finally, based on the above we can conclude that the discussion regarding the onset of the 'Anthropocene' (cf. Waters[44] and Kluiving[45]) can be alternatively described in more detail in the Dutch Late-Holocene soil and that in the western part of The Netherlands, it consists of several clearly distinguishable soil layers: moderate fine sand, weak silty, with unsorted debris and solid clay, weak silty, weak soily with little debris. The geological results combined with historical data in the research area reveal different anthropogenic substrate control in unique streets of Diemen. At this stage of our research, however, it is too soon to date the soil layers concerned more precisely than the beginning of the 1930s. We expect follow-up research will lead to better constrained and integrated geological and historical data focussing on events of the last 300 years.

Acknowledgements

We are most grateful to Bert Brouwenstijn and Joost van Ommen for their creative designs of Figures 2a-2c resp. Figure 7. Also we want to thank Tamme Stallinga of the Municipality of Diemen for his patient support when we were digging in the municipal Archives of Diemen. We are grateful to Jan Ronday for his photographic artworks. The paper benefitted greatly by reviews of Guillermo S. Reher and one anonymous reviewer.

---

42   J.R.A. Kattenberg, Geotechnisch en milieutechnisch onderzoek. Wegreconstructie Centrum West Diemen. Plan van aanpak. (Technisch onderzoeksrapport, MOS Grondmechanica, Rhoon 2015).
43   Diemer Archives INV. 5733: Bestek van gemeentelijke Dienst, 1935.
44   C. Waters et al., "The Anthropocene is distinct from the Holocene". Science 351 (2016): 6269, at 137.
45   S.J. Kluiving, S.J. & A. Hamel. Human niche construction as a perspective on the Anthropocene. RCC Perspectives: Transformations in Environment and Society. München, Germany , 2016.

References

Asselen, S. van. 2010. Peat compaction in deltas: Implications for Holocene delta evolution. Utrecht: University Press.

Blok, H., Krook, W., van Reenen, P. & Wiggers, R. (eds.) 2009 Diemen in het land van Amstel. Amsterdam: De Bataafsche Leeuw.

Bont, C. de. 2015. "Digging the river: the historical geography of the Amstel area (800-1275 AD)". Netherlands Journal of Geosciences 94, 353-63.

Gelder, R.S. van, Kluiving, S.J., Leemans, I.B., Ouden, R., & Goedhart, J. 2016. *Geological findings in unique streets of Diemen, The Netherlands, reveal different anthropogenic substrate control.* 4th International Landscape Archaeology Conference. Uppsala, Sweden.

Haskoning. 1994. Onderzoek betonnen wegconstructies – gemeente Diemen. Technisch onderzoeksrapport, Haskoning Koninklijk Ingenieursbureau, Nijmegen.

Haskoning. 1986. Onderzoek betonnen wegconstructies – Dienst gemeentewerken grondbedrijf Diemen. Technisch onderzoeksrapport, Haskoning Koninklijk Ingenieursbureau, Nijmegen.

Hellinga, P. 2013. Bestaande betonnen wegconstructie te Diemen. Beschouwing. Technisch onderzoeksrapport, Bartels, Leeuwarden.

Huizinga, T.K. & Dibbits, H.A.M.C. 1938. De ondergrond der wegen. Rapport, Association Internationale Permanente des Congrès de la Route, 's Gravenhage.

Kattenberg, J.R.A. 2015. Geotechnisch en milieutechnisch onderzoek. Wegreconstructie Centrum West Diemen. Plan van aanpak. Technisch onderzoeksrapport, MOS Grondmechanica, Rhoon.

Kluiving, S.J. & Hamel, A. 2016. Human niche construction as a perspective on the Anthropocene. RCC Perspectives: Transformations in Environment and Society. Münich, Germany.

Kluiving, S.J. & van Gelder, R.S. 2015. Geological investigation of the Gerardt Burghoutweg in Diemen, The Netherlands. Internal publication, Vrije Universiteit, Amsterdam.

Kluiving, S.J., van Gelder, R.S., Leemans, I.H. & Schmidt, F. 2017. 'What is the history of my house? An integrated approach between geology, archaeology, history and heritage studies.' *Geophysical Research Abstracts*. Vol. 19, EGU2017-18984.

Kooyman, H. (Lelystad, The Netherlands) resp. Rob Berkhout (Almere, The Netherlands): Personal messages: 26 april 2016

Koster, K. 2011. A geo-archaeological and historical geographical approach to examine 18th and 19th century pile driving in Amsterdam. Research master thesis Geoarchaeology, Vrije Universiteit, Amsterdam.

Krook, W. 2016. "Opgegraven schoeisel uit de 12e eeuw". Tijdschrift Historische Kring Diemen 26-2, 46-48, at 46.

Omegam. 1996. Technische Inspectie van een wijk op palen in Diemen. Technisch onderzoeksrapport, Onderzoeksdienst voor Milieu en Grondmechanica, Amsterdam.

Kuiper, E. 1946. Grondonderzoekingen en Betonberekeningen ter beantwoording van de vraag of weg no. 7 van het Rijkswegenplan 1938 tusschen de Beemsteruitwatering en de Weere ter lengte van 12 km., op een zandlichaam dan wel op palen dient te worden gefundeerd. Rapport Rijkswaterstaat, Directie Wegen.

Naber, J. 1999. "De Via Appia van de Lage Landen". ANWB-Kampioen 114-3, 104-107 at 104.

Schokker, J., Bakker, M.A.J., Dubelaar, C.W., Dombrink, R.M. & Harting, R. 2015. "3D subsurface modelling reveals the shallow geology of Amsterdam." Netherlands Journal of Geosciences, 94, 399-417, at 401

Smith, B.D. & Zeder, M.A. 2013. "The Onset of the Anthropocene." Anthropocene 4, 8-13.

Smolenaars, J.J.L. 2004. "Lofzang op een Romeinse snelweg: Statius Silv. IV". Lampas. Tijdschrift voor Nederlandse classici, 37, 122-142.

Steffen, W., Crutzen, P.J. & McNeill, J.R. 2007. "The Anthropocene: Are humans now overwhelming the great forces of Nature?" Ambio 36, 614-621.

Steffen, W., Broadgate, W., Deutsch, L., Gaffney, O. & Ludwig, C. 2015. "The trajectory of the Anthropocene: The Great Acceleration". The Anthropocene Review 2-1, 81-98. doi.org/10.1177/2053019614564785

Waters, C.N., Zalasiewicz, J., Summerhayes C., et al. 2016. "The Anthropocene is functionally and stratigraphically distinct from the Holocene". Science 351.

Vanoverbeke, R.W., Griffioen, A. & Smeerdijk, D. 2011. Archeologische opgraving 'Boerderij Landzigt' aan de Ouddiemerlaan te Diemen. Zaandijk: Hollandia archeologen, 11, 14.

Veerkamp, J.A.G., 2011. Terp-2; archeologische ontginningsterp Oud-Diemen. Research master thesis Archeologie, Vrije Universiteit, Amsterdam.

Archives of Municipality of Diemen

Diemer Archives (1931-1987), INV. 85 Correspondence Council 6 oktober 1933

Diemer Archives (1931-1987), INV. 85 Correspondence Council, 1935

Diemer Archives (1931-1987), INV. 85 Correspondence Council with Financial Department Haarlem, 6 april 1935.

Diemer Archives (1931-1987), INV. 85 Explanatory Memorandum B&W, 22 mei 1935

Diemer Archives INV. 5733: Bestek van gemeentelijke Dienst, 1935

Diemer Archives. Description on the backside of an undated and non-archived picture of the road. One of a series of pictures donated by the widow of the municipal building designer and clerk of the public works at that time, Jan de Boer.

Re-thinking Deep Time Landscapes

Christina Fredengren

a. Stockholm University, Department of Archaeology and Classical Studies, Sweden

Introduction

When the landscape concept re-entered archaeology (cf. Bender 1993, Knapp and Ashmore 1999) it was a new turn, as it placed human experience and action at the centre. Landscape was also a way of bringing together nature and culture so as to merge multiple sources of information into archaeological interpretations. As discussed by the human geographer, Tuan (1977, 89-90) in the 16th century, particularly in the Anglo-Saxon world, landscape referred to aesthetic scenery in art. Also, more importantly for Tuan, landscape is not what is "out there", in entities as trees, buildings or functional units, but it is more "a construct of the mind and feeling". Hence, landscapes were captured very much in the eye of the human beholder and modern landscape investigations paid attention to how humans have ordered space around them and imbued them with meaning (see also Cosgrove 1989, 120-127). Ingold (1993, 152) aimed at stitching together natural landscape as a backdrop and cultural landscape as symbolic and cognitive space through the focus on dwelling. In his view "the landscape is constituted as an enduring record of – and testimony to – the lives and works of past generations who have dwelt within it, and in so doing, have left there something of themselves.". While the intention was to follow how the world transforms itself (ibid 164) across nature and culture divides, in practice the focus was on following human task-scapes and activities that have crafted the environment. Furthermore, the past generations in question are mainly human and the reasoning handles (the human) perception of the environment. Denham (2017) states that "Landscape archaeology refers to the understanding of archaeological remains (artifacts, sites, and site complexes) in terms of the wider spatial realms (both physical and meaningful) of past human experience." Hence, human experience is placed at the center in standard landscape definitions.

The efforts of transgressing the nature/culture boundaries in heritage and landscape thinking has continued to be an important challenge, transgressed either as multi-natures or nature-cultures (see Lorimer 2012, Fredengren 2015), as the heritage making process is important for shaping a variety of futures in the selection process of what to pass on to future generations (Harrison 2015). With the emergence of the Anthropocene we have moved into what can be called a post-natural stage where most organisms, habitats, spaces and places have been infiltrated by human agencies and matters. In recent decades, however, both the human gaze and the relationships between humans and their surroundings have been explored in novel ways by feminist post-humanist thinkers and within the emerging fields of new materialism and the environmental humanities, challenging what it means to be a human and focusing on the relationship with the more-than human (cf. Hayward 2008, Haraway 2003, 2008, Barad 2007, Alaimo 2012, Braidotti 2013, 2018). These researchers study the human as coming into being through a variety of situated relations together with a range of other humans, animals and the environment. Hence, the human is always more-than-human and the human gaze is never human alone, but composed and entangled with a variety of other agents and agencies and this makes a difference for how to study landscapes. Also, the climate challenges of today have called into question continued anthropocentric visions of the future (cf. Haraway 2016), as such visions are much the reason for the troubles we are in today. Chakrabarty (2017, 41) writes "A single minded focus on human welfare and intra-human justice will most likely seem inadequate" and there is a need to include issues of survival of the more-than human, but also to develop a responsible stewardship of the planet.

The landscape concept is also powerful political tool, active within the heritage discourse, and used to mobilize resources as well as direct conservation and stewardship efforts. The landscape tool is tied to questions around what to keep, and what to let go of, remember and possibly mourn.

Critical posthumanist thinking and landscapes

This paper follows discussions in feminist post-humanist thinking that sometimes converge with and sometimes diverge from landscape as captured in the general heritage discourse. In order to see how these ideas could breathe new life into old issues is an effort to face up to the current climate and environmental predicaments.

This paper re-works traditional approaches to archaeological/natural landscape analyses through feminist environmental humanities theory. Hence, it provides additions to the understanding of landscapes from being captured primarily by human perception and meaningmaking, to being composed and in process of change due to the activities of many more-than-human agentialities.

It deals with questions of how landscapes could be approached differently if the anthropocentric focus was lessened, in ways that would open up discussions of deep-time, more-than-human visions, temporality, responsibility and care, where not only human, but also multispecies survival is at stake.

This will be done by using for example the writings of Rose et. Al (2012), Haraway (2016) and Barad (2007, 2012), but also other researchers such as time-philosopher Bastian (2012, 2017), that without explicitly articulating it, deals with materiality, temporality and matters akin to what is captured in landscape and heritage discourses, and could be enrolled to discuss landscapes of human and more-than humans and change how to approach issues of conservation and stewardship. These authors (Rose et. Al 2012; Haraway 2016; Bastian 2012, 2017) also engage in issues around social justice in the environmental humanities and could be useful to exemplify what such landscape approaches could be like. Some of this research I have drawn upon in earlier works (Fredengren 2013, 2015, 2016) that also will provide entry points for the current paper.

This paper raises the following questions:

- How could we relate to landscape in new ways through the environmental humanities and feminist post-humanism in ways that moves beyond anthropocentrism and includes the more-than-human?
- What implications would this have for how to approach issues of time and intra-generational justice and care?
- What components and questions would a landscape approach relate to, in order to move towards an approach that is more fit to the current environmental dilemmas, and that to a larger degree is sensitive to and pay attention to deep time relations and to processes of intra-generational justice and care?

This is of particular importance as landscape concepts have since made its way into major treaties, such as the European Landscape Convention (ELC). This entered into force in 2004 and is an important instrument in natural and cultural heritage policies in Europe and manages human impact on the physical landscape in Europe. Furthermore, to place the human being as the ethical centre, as some of the landscape approaches tend to do, may be particularly challenging in times described as the "anthropocene". This epoch has been described as times when humans are identified as one of the main agents in earth system change, when human actions collectively became a global geological force in their own right (Crutzen & Stoermer 2000), with alarming effects on humans, animals, environment and climate. Hence it is of importance to gather forces elsewise and to possibly adjust and re-think deep-time landscapes in order to deal better with climate and environmental challenges.

More-than-human landscapes

The term landscape emerged in an early stage of capitalism and was connected with a particular, often male, elitist, way of seeing and experiencing the surrounding (see also Bollig 2009, Widgren 2015 who deal with the concept in depth). This type of landscape view was challenged and it was pointed out that instead is something that is experienced, altered through historical conditions, contested and negotiated, which it how it more recently have been used in landscape scholarship (cf. Bender 1993). A renewed landscape theory and method came into the archaeological field as a way of paying attention to the contexts of archaeological sites, but also to how the various human creators/observers were situated and involved with place making. The landscape concept (cf. Tuan 1979, Bender 1993, Knapp & Ashmore 1999) brought people back into the equation and presented a forum of discussing how gendered, ethicized or class-distinguished landscapes may have differed from each other and be used for contestations of power. Landscape analysis combined in focus both geographical and social situatedness, where for example Ingold (1993, 152-3) proposed that knowledge of a landscape can be obtained through *dwelling* *i.e.* by participating and practicing a range of tasks and activities in a landscape. Here, landscape thinking resembles what was described some years earlier by Donna Haraway (1988, 583ff) as situated knowledge, *i.e.* that knowledge (including landscape knowledge) is always produced by an embodied someone who is situated in hierarchies, knowledge communities and in place. This is by Haraway contrasted against knowledge constructed from above, as performing a so called "god trick", that sees everywhere from nowhere. A landscape archaeology that draws on both these traditions would work with such situated, embodied knowledge domains that come about by paying close attention to a particular place and drawing on an engagement with the environment. The term landscape has also worked as a measure towards integration of natural and cultural elements in the heritage analysis (cf. Olwig & Lowenthal 2006:4).

It has also become a politically powerful tool that is defined by the European Landscape Convention (ELC):

> *"Landscape" means an area, as perceived by people, whose character is the result of the action and interaction of natural and/or human factors.*

Widgren (2015, 202) has noted that the convention's origin in scenic understanding of landscape, linked to Anglo-French ideas, which differ from the more territorial connotations in Nordic languages. Furthermore, the landscape concept is both in its territorial and scenic aspect anthropocentric as it places certain people´s perceptions center-stage. Nature and culture is bridged by the human gaze. The material features of a landscape may be described, but it is how they are perceived, their meaning and valuation by people, and the contribution to their welfare that matters. What gets pushed to the side is the study of what relations come together through how bodies and materialities weave in and out of each other over longer periods of time, for both human and more-than-human animals (Fredengren 2015). A landscape thinking that places the human as set apart from nature and materiality risks to downplay other agencies as well as push such ontologies on other groups (Head 2012:65-69) and importantly may bring out ways of dealing with landscapes that isolates human well-being from that of other species in the environment. In this context it is worth noting how Ingold in 2016 describes his (1993) paper, as an experiment with the landscape concept that failed, as it focused more on humans being-in-the world, instead of exploring a variety of relationalities within the environment. Ingold (2016, 31) has since been inspired by the feminist post-human philosopher Barad (2007) to follow the differential becoming of the inhabitants of the earth and we will take this reasoning a bit further below. An alternative approach would comprise studies of relations and reciprocities between human and non-human actors in landscapes as living-webs (Harrison & Rose 2010:251) and as an addition to investigate how such relationships form over longer periods of time and may stretch into distant futures, where inheritances of all kinds bring about differentiated worldings. The climate challenges of today needs new deep-time understanding and action Chakrabarty (2009/2017) and they also need new approaches to landscapes elsewise as compared to the way landscapes are portrayed in ELC.

Whereas landscape thinking of Tuan and others described the landscape as being creations of human meaning making, perceptions and actions, there are other ways of working with relations with the environment, from within the human body and beyond, that are developing within the environmental humanities. Rose et al. (2012) advise 'thinking through the environment' and thereby to explore how human attentiveness to the world is expanded by allying with a variety of environmental agents and agencies. Hence, new parts of reality can unfold through acknowledging shared human, non-human ontologies, through engaging with and paying close attention to those agents, often separated out as nature or environment. This could occur through exploring how perception changes through exploring how human-animal relations change perception. For example, Hayward (2010:592-3) examines how corals and starfish encounter the environment. Their arms have "finger-eyes" that make out their sensorial capacities when they engage with the world. Hayward calls this developing a "*zoo-indexicality*" where the animal and researcher becomes" a sensorial ensemble, becoming more than ourselves" providing an affordance of "intercorporeality" that re-tunes human perception and the ways that the world presents itself (Hayward 2008). This could for example be about how wetland landscapes were explored "on the hoof", where human bodies were co-working with cattle bodies in an intercorporeality in the practice of herding across wetland landscape, that would bear out in, and be marked by Bronze Age placemaking (cf. Fredengren & Löfqvist 2015). The human-animal co-working brought about a material worlding of the landscape, that highlighted certain places of passage. Alaimo (2010:2, 22) has explored how the boundary between the body and its surroundings are blurred; "biology and politics merge as people, places and substances merge." Here, the human body is understood as *transcorporeal*, always situated and composed through a range of relations that makes it more-than-human. Likewise, there is an urge to think through things (cf. Henare, Holbraad & Wastell 2007) which could be understood as a type of "material-indexicality" where heritage sites and monuments can be understood as assemblages that gather the world around them in situated ways. To add another strand to the "thinking through" assemblage, we could consider what would happen if we would "think through the temporalities of the environment" and pay more attention to various types of material-temporal-indexicalites that are important in how landscapes fold out through time.

Taken together, zoo-indexicality, material-indexicality, trancscorporeality or time-indexicalities, could encourage heritage practitioners to move beyond human perception and to see how material heritages, but also how living together with the more-than-human, such as animals and vegetation in a historic environment indexes and points to intricate ways of interspecies co-habitation embedded in the environment. Hence, landscape heritage can be used as apparatuses to re-shape thought and bring inspiration to alternative practices and relations to be enrolled in sustainable action.

The past is not what it used to be (but neither are the presents or the futures)

Heritage has been understood as an attributed label, "Heritage" applied politically to things, places and practices from the past in the present (Smith 2006) and has recently mainly been studied through social constructivist perspectives. Hence, heritage does not deal so much with the past as it used to do, it is more about political processes in the present. Hence, heritagemaking can be understood as producing a "presentism", an ever present now, which is a particular historically situated way of experiencing time in late modern times (cf. Hartog 2017 (2003)). The scrutiny of the heritage concept in critical heritage studies (see Smith 2006) has been beneficial to expose the injustices in how such classification are carried out and where inequalities based on gender, class and ethnicity have created a hegemonical, authorized heritage discourse and selection of places, focusing on the use of heritage in identity politics. The landscape concept, as a part of the heritage label repertoire, can likewise also be seen as constructed in the present, through the modern human gaze, to describe what ought to be valued and kept in a landscape and what is allowed to change. However, these matters are much more complex than this. As argued elsewhere (Fredengren 2015) by making use of Barad's process ontology (2007, 2012) to label something as heritage is to make an agential cut into an ever-changing world. Here, heritage can be understood as a material-semiotic phenomena to be investigated as a doing, that comes about through intra-active processes, differentiating and diffracting through time. However, heritage comes into place both due to selection practices separating heritage from non-heritage, but also "matter" matters in this process. Hence to capture heritage as a phenomena is different as compared to how heritage and landscapes are handled when only seen as existing and coming into place through the eye of the beholder and expressed as due to language constructions by humans. The focus would move from how humans perceive the landscape to a folding out of how various changing relations and framings makes it come into worlding as multi-temporal places together with the more-than-human.

But even if we would strictly adhere to the view that heritage labelling deals mainly with the present, the labelling addresses materialities that have a variety of material and temporal trajectories, that tend to break out of the presentist mould. As discussed by Lucas (2015) and Olivier (2011) following Serres and Latour (1995, 58-60), the present is infiltrated by a number of materialities of different time-depths. As suggested by Lucas, the past, present and future do not follow each other as successive features, instead materialities of different times, meet, touch and fold together in non-chronolinear-ways. Some of these have a duration over thousands of years, and have been related to by many different generations, others that have been concealed in the sediments, decay in our hands, when exposed to air and lose their durability, but not always without affecting us (see Fredengren 2016). Labelled and classified or unclassified heritage materialities support the landscape with different paces, rhythms and durance, where some are in processes of abandonment, disrepair and decay. What Barad (2007, 2012, 32) adds to this question is the queerness of time, that materialisation processes of both pasts and futures are constantly set in relation to each other, they are "iteratively reworked" through what is called "space-time-mattering". In effect landscapes may hold a variety of materializing potentialities, some shaped to a degree by humans, others not, but the point is that there is always an ongoing entanglement, that produce past, present, futures in connection with each other and even diffracting into each other's. Take for example oil that has formed through the deposition of dead organisms over millions of years, who's use and abuse in the modern period creates a series of relationships that will affect generations to come, by damaging the climate or being used in plastic industry. Many megalithic tombs have in their monumentality been present since the Neolithic period and have been related to both materially and immaterially over time, some soils have grown to a depth of c. 20 cm since the Bronze Age and due to the assemblage of a variety of agencies, become fertile and crop bearing, some open landscapes became such during the Iron Age, while other archaeological features have just peaked-through the soil surface due to development excavations. A variety of features make out the fabric of the landscape that is in constant process of developing and entangling in new ways. These materialites and materialisation processes can be considered *as deep-time interventions* (a term here credited to David Farrier at Edinburgh University) that has effects for many generations to come.

Landscape heritage and conservation most often do not deal with such processes, but focus on the "finitude of human creation" of worlds to be lost or remnants of lost worlds. However, in the Anthropocene, when the said anthropos shifts materials around the earth, this force also creates new heritage, that rarely are acknowledged as such. For example, as pointed out by Bastian & Van Doreen, it has set materials like plastic, toxins and radioactivity in new circulations that may have effects over vast periods and cause irreparable mass-extinctions across species boundaries. These moves also have temporal effects that impinge on the future, and work outside the ordinary life-span of a human. This change has come about for example through manufacturing, agriculture or energy industries that are all "time – and place bending" and that has set a variety of force and temporalities in motion (Bastian & Van Doreen 2017). Also, these shifts make or break a variety of material and immaterial ties in the landscape, such ties have a variety of temporalities and affect times ahead, some of them working from deep time pasts, others into deep time futures. Here, landscape studies could gain from paying attention to such time and place bending processes and materialities.

This is where there is scope for landscape archaeology to change landscape action and thinking and place relations to materiality and temporality more in focus as this is of importance for facing the challenges of climate change, environmental decay, multispecies extinction and how to go beyond anthropocentric visions. Chakrabarty (2017, 42) has drawn attention to how the sciences provide evidence for deep time connections between biological and geological processes on the planet, and these will in turn form the basis for the engagement of social sciences in environmental issues. This means to contextualize humans in a much deeper history of planetary life. However, this may not necessarily be a question of "zooming out" to geological times (Bastian & Van Doreen 2017, 5). Many different material and immaterial processes stretch and entangle through the present, both in expected and unexpected ways.

While the past may not be what it used to be, the present is no longer, flatly the present, as in heritage theory. Haraway (2016, 101) writes that it is important to be "situating ourselves within complex, multivalent, temporalities". The materialisation processes of time and landscape are instead rather queer. They consist of a variety of jumbled up temporalities, for example geological, biological, archaeological and social, working in webs of deep time landscapes. Here, they contribute to temporal diversity in the landscape.

New immortals and double deaths

These are times when older certainties and stabilities, such as the Holocene climate or the relationships between and composition of species, are breaking down. At the same time, there are a variety of materials, where "the finitude of human creation" is not as certain, but where substances are brought to play and have been put into unceasing circulation. Among these are, for example, toxic chemicals, pollution, plastics and radioactive waste that have all become new immortals in the environment as human actions are stretched out way further than human lifetimes (Bastian & Van Doreen 2017, 1). Human induced climate change also has a variety of chain-effects, such as ice-melts, changes of sea currents (think only of the thermohaline that transports water around the globe in 1000-year cycles) as well as anticipated water-level rises that will eventually submerge large areas of archipelagoes and coastal areas. There are multi-species worlds that will be lost through rising sea-levels (even if we stop at the 2 degrees of global warming, this is a process that has been started and will continue with force due to this). These, and other material developments caused by human hands could also be classified as a type of landscape cultural heritage, albeit of the more unwanted kind. However, such heritages of environmental and multispecies dangers, have often have been left out in discussions of authorized heritage discourse, neither have they been handled to any extent by the heritage agencies (more than as a threat to built heritage, that is being conserved to last, if not for eternity as was thought in early days of conservation, at least for a foreseeable future).

As Bastian & VanDoreen writes, there are indeed worlds to be lost as "old immortals" are on their way out, and new ones percolate their way in. The issue at stake is when "mortals acts and creations" take on a temporality that is next to immortal, with effects for both humans and more-than-humans for generations to come. While there is no such immortality, there are ongoing processes of where these substances of endurance intersect with and have relations with other life-processes (Bastian & VanDoreen 2017, 4). Hence, there are worlds in the making, of pollution, extinction and irreparable damage to the environment, that will be hard to undo, but also a variety of new processes that will strike by surprise.

This extended life of the new "immortals" is contrasted by Bastian & VanDoreen to what has been called *double death*. While there is death that occur as parts of the life-cycle, double death takes place at a rate where there are no ways for recuperation of ecosystems, where death is amplified so that the life-death balance is damaged (Bird Rose 2012). These double deaths and immortalities are acted out in landscapes of complex, materializing temporalities. There are lost worlds that may lie dormant/latent/come to the fore as temporal entanglement of different paces, practices and phases that will bind temporalities together and cause double deaths for times ahead and will work as expected or unexpected interventions. Climate change is in this respect the grand heritage of the Anthropocene period that will affect human and more-than human generations over vast amounts of time!

Intragenerational justice and care

Acknowledging that landscape and heritage are politically used concepts, we cannot turn a blind eye to the fact that this is politics that enacts a brokering function between generations, that also work as temporal interventions, that bends both time and space in particular ways. Today both natural and cultural heritage institutions have responsibilities that make intergenerational trade-offs *i.e.* deals with resource-allocations between generations. However, how, and according to what principles such deliberations are done is less than clear. Taylor (2013) shows that the ideologies of what heritage to preserve for the future, resemble, but do not draw on traditional and more well-known theories of intergenerational justice such as those presented by Rawls (1971). Rawls´ formed the classic definitions of sustainability, such as that of the Brundtland commission (UN 1987) that strives to ensure that resource usage in the present does not hamper future choices for, primarily, humans. Against this background, it is notable that representatives of the cultural heritage sector have a rather vague articulation of which futures may benefit from safeguarded heritage (Högberg 2016) or how heritage could be enrolled for more hopeful futures to come for humans and more-than-humans.

The designing of time, and trade-offs on which generation´s time is counted and whose time is not, comes to the fore in climate issues and sustainable development. The issues of how to handle responsibilities and care between generations is of major importance in the transitions to sustainable futures. That heritage has links to more sustainable living and contributes to social, economic and environmental development has been discussed by many (see Fredengren 2012). However, there has been less discussion of how heritage ties in with the formation of temporalities, and questions of justice between past-, present- and future generations and when visions of sustainable futures clash or when they contradict the common economic development narratives.

Here, the constructivist turn on landscape has beneficially critiqued how such heritage classification have been dealt with and sometimes created injustices within generations; where gender, class and ethnicity biases have been reinforced by unequal discourse and in selections of sites and monuments. However, these discussions have arisen from a perspective that places the human being at the center and issues about how justice and care in-between generations is dealt with less frequency and have often been left un-problematized (Fredengren 2015). Issues about what responsibilities there are towards the unborn often have been dealt with within climate justice discussions, but as argued by for example Chakrabarty, we can no longer afford the luxury of keeping the social sciences "obsessively human centered", but need to go beyond both species and temporal boundaries in thoughts and actions (2017, 40-42). Hence, landscape heritage deliberations need to take into account temporal issues of the lives, deaths and conviviality of both humans and more-than-humans, instead of primarily focusing on human wellbeing, for considering the variety of life-forms and processes that compose the landscapes.

As argued above, if the past, neither the present are what they used to be, there might be a chance to re-work landscapes as materializing multi-temporal time-givers, that are more in tune with what is going on and what to do about it. Here Bastian´s discussions of temporalities and clocks could be useful. Bastian (2012,

31) defines a clock as "a device that signals change in order for its users to maintain an awareness of, and thus be able to coordinate themselves with, what is significant to them. (…) Further, each clock can be read as an affirmation of a shared social relation *to* something – to the layering of rocks, to the sun, to a particular type of atom. Rather than measuring a disembodied time, clocks become profoundly material." To listen to the material clocks of landscapes would require us to pay close attention to materialization processes that criss-cross and diffract across time – some with slower rhythms, other with fast paces, some that spread out in space-time, others that contract or twist time for a variety of species becomings. There would then be a need to analyze landscapes with questions such: as whose temporalities do we pay attention to and who is asked to stand back, particularly in human induced projects, such as infrastructural investments or change of land-use. That would mean to focus more on how various life- and death times interconnected with each other – which would, using Bastian´s words, contribute to "a new awareness of how we are related to each other" in the landscape. Instead of analyzing landscapes as chrono-linear-time occurrences, with a before, during and after development, changes need to be argued and thought through in relation to a number of different conflicting temporal trajectories (backwards, forwards, emerging, decaying, punctuated etc). That would then enable us to pay closer attention more to relational time and how materiality and immateriality co-work between generations and what difference landscapes could give for conviviality across multi-species generations.

From geneaological ancestry to making kin

Haraway´s (2011) paper (that thinks through the artwork of Piccinini) deals with issues of how to take care of unexpected, and sometimes, blasted country and how to learn to inherit well. The paper delivered a critique of the salvation histories of western conservation practices that sometimes strive for the restoration of the pristine and the past as it was or seem to have been. However, many people today live in post-industrial landscapes, affected by modernization and technological development. Most live in technocultures and "must study how to live in actual places, cultivate practices of care, and risk ongoing face-to-face encounters with unexpected partners". Haraway here refers to an aboriginal way of relating to time and responsibility, to face the past, committing to letting the present flourish, and thereby backing into the future with the ancestor, rather than hinging the lived time between a past and a future. These ancestors however, may well be queerly related species, that greet us and urge us to relate to time and material processes in unconventional ways.

Whereas it is often emphasised that indigenous people around the world have an immense ancestral knowledge of how to engage with land and waters in more respectful ways (cf. Strang 2007, Hikuroa 2017). Besides that, landscapes are undergoing constant change, many indigenous and non-indigenous people have been displaced and lost the connection with such knowledges of the land, due to for example migration and urbanisation. There is a need for exploring how to develop such knowledge while moving to new places or for getting on in under altered climatic circumstances. Here landscape and archaeology have something in particular to offer. Haraway, suggests that the way forward is "to make kin", which is an alternative for an engagement with ancestry, that questions ancestry as mainly directed by genealogy. There is a need to disentangle these two, kin and ancestry, from each other, and instead approach kin as a sympoesis that makes up persons, but not necessarily only as human individuals (2016, 102-3). Ancestry is a concept that can be used politically for othering and therefore needs to be critically scrutinized. Engaging with landscape heritages, or with archaeological artefacts, could be a way of making kin or for forging material ancestralities with the surroundings – to pay close attention to materialization processes and to figure out which worlds are worlding through the material/temporal indexicalities of things, places and environments. Such knowledge has the potential to provide ways to tune into how situated places are entangled and might provide means for to explore it also for people not familiar with the land. This could also work as an entry port to ways of accessing and tapping into forgotten indigenous knowledge, to find kind/kin in the human and more-than-human ancestors of the land, without necessarily having a genealogical ancestry connection to place.

In heritage of all kinds (labelled or not) there is material learning and ways of making contact with all sorts of materialising ancestors, or perhaps rather kindred's. Such inheritances could be useful to approach and build attachments with material, immaterial, human and more-than-humans in the landscape). As discussed in Fredengren (2015) for example, paying close attention to old buildings is a way of folding them out as material relatings and relata, they can hold material clues for how to get on in a landscape, where to find wood-supplies for building, water, safe dwelling or grazing in the environment or how to avoid hazards. Also, artefacts, settlements or other features, are to a certain extent transcorporeal, where materials and locations may be used as material indexes, as small maps of localised worlds, that point out how they draw on relations to other places in the wider landscapes for example through their dependency on materials from other locations. To a certain extent, they may summon a variety of temporal indices in their materiality. Here, they also go through cycles of birth, flourishing and decay, but often have a different and longer life-span than people and continue to be a part of the life-webs of generations to come. Hence such inheritances are traces that show the complex ways in which lives are entangled and impressed in each other over time.

Rose et al 2017 engage in issues about the importance of practicing care and responsibility over generations. But with whom and with what ethics do you engage in such care? Chakrabarty (2017, 41) has started to explore these questions, where for example the biblical narrative states that humans are set to dominate the earth, but Pope Francis has recently argued that this should not be misunderstood as sovereignty, but the human is to work with care as a gardener, or a responsible steward. Also, Haraway (2011) suggests we approach conservation issues, with a different twist, where practicing of care for country could be approached as if being a surrogate parent. "Parenting is about caring for generations, one's own or not; reproducing is about making more of oneself to populate the future, quite a different matter. Here it is about being well-tuned-in and actively near the land for it to flourish, but not necessarily to set back landscape to some pristine past to "heal the scars of the modern and technological", that would be the goal for the salvationists, but to engage in the temporally messy compositions of the now. Haraway (2011) writes: "To parent is to instruct, guard, carry, nurture and finally let go." Or as in Haraway (2016, 10-11, 131) not about restoration or reconciliation but a commitment to a more modest possibility of responding to others, to practice "response-ability" and to stay with the troubles of finding ways of getting on together or to find partial recuperation. Where Haraway (2016, 102) talks of how to make kin sympoetically (to make with each other), Barad, similarly, queries a metaphysiscs based on differences between inter-action that applies to cooperation between individual entities and process ontologies where objects do not exist before relations are in place (2012:30-33). This approach could also be useful when teasing out issues of inter- and intra-generational justice and care, to point to how we make presents or perhaps even presensings in situated ways based on relations with others of varying time depths and temporalities.

The art of composing, composting and letting go

Drawing on the reasoning above, there may be no real "immortals" in the landscapes, as old ones are on the way out and new ones enters the scene. However, an increasing number of landscape locations could be described as wounded places, where refuges are decreasing and where both species and temporal diversity is altered. In many, development affected landscapes, certain lives and materialities are sacrificed on behalf of what is understood as the common or commercial good (Reinert 2015). At the same time, the so-called heritage industry is often characterized and criticized for engaging in hoarding practices, taking up storage-space, threatening to cause an overflow of objects, that could cause a heritage-infarct of systemic kind (Ola Wetterberg personal communication). However, whilst hoarding might not always be the solution, many of these places with their broken relations go without acknowledgement, and irreversible losses pass without official ceremonies of mourning, or artefacts and samples decay slowly in museum storage. These are places where the art of letting go is practiced, but possibly not marked to any greater extent. Whereas DeSilvey (2017, 5) in the book curated decay, writes that "decay and disintegration can be culturally (as well as ecologically) productive", there is a challenge of how to make such productivity come to fore. These may be places where the existential side of heritages needs to be dealt with, where "the finitute of human creation", lost world and the limited life-span of humans would deserve to be reflected upon.

As Haraway writes (2016, 69) there is a need for memory workers to act as speakers for the dead *i.e.* "to bring the dead into the present, so to make more response-able living and dying possible in times yet to come." Taken into landscape thinking, this suggests a task and responsibility not only in the deliberation process leading up to landscape change to ask how we "are at stake to each other" (p. 55) as humans and more-than-humans, but also in the aftermath of change, where there is a need to facilitate arenas where to mourn losses, to see how "order can be re-knitted" and how practice hospitality/response to human and more-than-human others and learn to inherit well.

Haraway (2016, 101) writes "Renewed generative flourishing cannot grow from myths of immortality or failure to become with the dead and extinct". Climate change will also amplify the amount of places that will become uninhabitable and increase the need for practices of both mourning losses and to be creative about how to continue to live. Landscape heritages may be for more than preserving what once was – but may work as ways for figuring out and how to get on in particularly situated landscape, over several multi-species and material generations. In engaging in landscape heritages of variously naturally and culturally entangled ways, there is a need for a focus on practices around the art of letting go and to become with the dead and the extinct in new ways. This is one field where archaeology and deep time landscape studies matter and for this to provide a material storytelling of the dead, for letting go or mourning losses, but more importantly to deal with complex ways of how to co-habit with both past, present and future generations, as well as to heal wounded landscapes by thinking through unruly deep time entanglements and kin-based intra-generational justice and care.

Conclusions

This paper has started to draft a landscape approach in conversation with the scholarship that is emerging in the environmental humanities and feminist post-humanism. While both landscape heritage studies and these scholars have the focus on tracing out situated social injustices, the differences lie in the focus on the human and how the factor of materialising time is treated. In heritage studies, the focus is often in the present, while scholarship in the environmental humanities is increasingly interested in both deep time pasts and long-term effects into the future. Furthermore, heritage studies of the social constructivist type often place human perception and experience in the centre. Here critical post-humanists have started to explore ways of dealing with a world that does not place selective human well-being as the ethical center, and explore what it would be like if life-cycles, paces and temporalities of a range of more-than-human others instead as well materialities were observed.

These approaches offer new, situated ways to relate to landscapes, beyond landscapes as captured by the human gaze alone. Instead landscapes could be understood as a jumble up of materialities in process of becoming something else, but at different paces and different speeds, where heritagemaking of landscapes, bring out phenomena that are interventions and agential cuts into these evolving textures that on some occasions shape the course of events for considerable expanses of time. Here, temporalities of the landscape could be explored, just as Ingold suggests by dwelling and carrying out tasks in the landscape. However, in addition to this there is a need to engage and respond to the processes in place and for to pay close attention to immaterializing and materializing forces at play in situated location. This in order for to see what these places offers in the landscape to different human and more-than human others and how such brings about different types of worlding. It is more a question of how to better re-tie the material and immaterial knots between past, present and future generations, and to suggest ways forward for moving towards innovative ways of checking in with our post-natural and materializing clocks. This approach provides opportunities for investigations of temporalities, materiality and ethics and how they fold and diffract into a variety of futures in new ways. Besides dwelling in the landscape, it is urgent to pay attention to such time and place bending processes that alter the living condition for many species on the planet, as well as to deal with justices and injustices already written into the fabric of the world.

This reasoning would also have implications for how to approach issues of inter- and intragenerational justice and care, as it would point towards both relations of interdependencies between material- and multi-species generations. Here considerations and engagement beyond genealogical ancestry, but more with deep-time kin making is warranted. It would also point towards analysis of where such relations are violated, broken and sacrificed and the need to take time carrying out ceremonies of mourning of losses, wounded landscapes, sacrifices, double deaths and to pay close attention to the tricks carried out by the new immortals. Landscapes are also places, where to learn also from what could be termed adopted and materialising more-than-human ancestors about how to recuperate, practice hospitality and how to inherit well, as well as sometimes, to participate in celebrations and joy felt in practicing in the art of letting go. With the ongoing climate crisis there is a need to develop practices and perhaps even rituals to mark out and handle both worlds in the making and worlds about to be lost.

Acknowledgements

This paper is a development the topic of DeepTime and the collaboration with the SeedBox, the Posthumanities hub and Stockholm University Environmental Humanities network. Formas funding for the project Checking in with Deep Time – intragenerational justice and care is gratefully acknowledged, where this paper is a preamble to the project. Thanks also go to the advice of my reviewers that have improved this paper immensely, anonymous and Guillermo S. Reher.

References

Alaimo, S. 2010. *Bodily Natures: Science, Environment, and the Material Self.* Indiana: Indiana University Press.

Barad, K. 2007. *Meeting the Universe Halfway.* Durham and London: Duke University Press.

Barad, K. 2012. Nature's Queer Performativity. *Kvinder, Køn & Forskning* Vol. 1-2, 25-53.

Bastian, M. 2017. Liberating clocks: developing a critical horology to rethink the potential of clock time. In New Formations. Special Issue: Timing Transformations.

Bastian, M. 2012. Fatally Confused: Telling the Time in the Midst of Ecological

Crises. Environmental Philosophy 9(1), 23-48.

Bastian, M. & van Doreen, T. 2017. The New Immortals: Immortality and Infinitude in the Anthropocene. *Environmental Philosophy* 14:1, 1-9.

Bender, B. (ed,) 1993. *Landscape: politics and perspectives.* Oxford: Berg.

Bollig, M. 2009. Visions of landscape: an introduction. In Bollig, M. & Bubenzer, O. (eds.) *African landscapes: interdisciplinary approaches* (Vol. 4). New York: Springer Science & Business Media, 1-40.

Chakrabarty, D. 2009. The Climate of History: Four Theses, *Critical Inquiry* 2009:2, vol. 35.

Chakrabarty, D. 2017. The future of the human sciences in the age of humans: A note. *European Journal of Social Theory.* Vol. 20(1), 39-43.

Crutzen, P.J. & E.F. Stoermer, 2000. The 'Anthropocene'. *Global Change Newsletter* 41, 17.

Denham, T. 2016. Landscape Archaeology. In Gilbert, A.S. (ed.) Encyclopedia of Geoarchaeology. Encyclopedia of Earth Sciences Series. Springer, Dordrecht.

DeSilvey, C. 2017. *Curated Decay: Heritage beyond Saving.* Minneapolis: University of Minnesota Press.

Fredengren, C. 2016. Deep time enchantment. Bog bodies, crannogs and other worldly sites at disjuncture's in time. Archaeology and Environmental Ethics. *World Archaeology* 48:4.

Fredengren, C. 2015. Nature: cultures: Heritage, Sustainability and Feminist Posthumanism. *Current Swedish Archaeology*, 23, 109-130.

Fredengren, C. & Löfqvist, C. 2015. Food for Thor. The deposition of human and animal remains in a Swedish wetland area. *Journal of Wetland Archaeology* 15, 122-48.

Fredengren, C. 2013. Posthumanism, the transcorporeal and biomolecular archaeology. *Current Swedish Archaeology*, Vol. 21, 53-71.

Fredengren, C. 2012. Kulturarvets värde för en hållbar samhällsutveckling. In Fredengren, C., Jensen, O.W. & Wall, Å. (eds.) *I valet och kvalet: Grundläggande frågor kring värdering och urval av kulturarvet.* Stockholm: Riksantikvarieämbetet, 189-224.

Haraway, D. 1988. Situated knowledges: the science question in feminism and the privilege of partial perspective. Feminist studies. 14(3), 575-599.

Haraway, D. 2011. Speculative Fabulations for Technoculture's Generations: Taking

Care of Unexpected Country. Australian Humanities Review. Issue 50, May 2011, 1-18.

Haraway, D. 2016. *Staying With the Trouble: Making Kin in the Chtulucene.* Durham: Duke University Press.

Harrison, R. & Rose, D. 2010. Intangible Heritage. In Benton, T. (ed.) *Understanding Heritage and Memory.* Manchester & New York: Manchester University Press, 238-276.

Hartog, F. 2015. Regimes of Historicity. Presentism and Experiences of Time. New York: Columbia University Press.

Hayward, E. 2008. More Lessons from a Starfish: Prefixial Flesh and Trans-speciated Selves. WSQ: *Women's Studies Quarterly.* Vol. 36 (3-4), 64-85.

Hayward, E. 2010. Fingereyes: Impressions of Cup Corals. *Cultural Anthropology.* Vol. 25. Issue 4, 577-599.

Hikuroa, D. 2017. Mātauranga Māori – the ūkaipō of knowledge in New Zealand, Journal of the Royal Society of New Zealand, 47:1, 5-10.

Head, L. 2012. Conceptualising the Human in Cultural Landscapes and Resilience Thinking. In Plieninger, T., & Bieling, C. (eds.) *Resilience and the Cultural Landscape: Understanding and Managing Change in Human-Shaped Environments:* 65-79. Cambridge: Cambridge University Press.

Henare, A., Holbraad, M. & Wastell, S. 2007. Thinking through Things. In Henare, A., Holbraad, M. & Wastell, S. (eds.) *Thinking through Things: Theorising Artefacts Ethnographically.* London: Routledge.

Ingold, T. 1993. The temporality of the landscape. *World Archaeology*, 25(2), 152-174.

Ingold, T. 2016. Archaeology with Its Back to the World. *Norwegian Archaeological Review.* Vol. 49, No. 1, 30-32.

Knapp, B.A. & Ashmore, W. 1999. "Archaeological Landscapes: Constructed, Conceptualized, Ideational". In Ashmore, W. & Knapp, B.A. (eds.) *Archaeologies of Landscape*. Malden: Blackwell Publishers.

Lorimer, J. 2012. Multinatural geographies for the Anthropocene. *Progress in Human Geography* 36(5), 593-612.

Lucas, G. 2015. Archaeology and Contemporaneity. *Archaeological Dialogues* 22 (1), 1-15.

Olivier, L. 2011. *The Dark Abyss of Time. Archaeology and Memory.* Altamira Press: London and New York.

Olwig, K.R. & Lowenthal, D. 2006. *The Nature of Cultural Heritage and the Culture of Natural Heritage: Northern Perspectives on a Contested Patrimony.* London & New York: Routledge.

Reinert, H. 2015. Sacrifice. *Environmental Humanities* Vol 7, 255-258.

Rose, D.B. 2012. Multispecies Knots of Ethical Time. Environmental Philosophy 9(1), 127-140.

Rose, D.B., van Dooren, T. & Chrulew, M. 2017. *Extinction Studies: Stories of Time, Death and Generations*, Columbia University Press: New York.

Rose, D.B., van Dooren, T., Chrulew, M., Cooke, S., Kearnes, M. & Gorman, E. 2012. Thinking through the Environment, Unsettling the Humanities. *Environmental Humanities,* vol. 1, 1-5.

Serres, M. & Latour, B. 1995. *Conversations on Science, Culture and Time.* Ann Arbor: The University of Michigan Press.

Smith, L.J. 2006. *Uses of Heritage.* New York: Routledge.

Strang, V. 1997. *Uncommon Ground: Cultural landscapes and environmental values*. Oxford: Berg.

Rawls, J. 1971. *A Theory of Justice.* Massachusettes: Harvard University Press.

Taylor, A. 2013. Intergenerational Justice: A Useful Perspective for Heritage Conservation. *CeROArt*. https://ceroart.revues.org/3510.

Tuan, Y. 1977. *Space and Place: The Perspective of Experience*. Minneapolis: University of Minnesota Press.

UN1987. *Report of the World Commission on Environment and Development: Our Common Future. Brundtland Report*. United Nations Assembly. Session 42.

Widgren, M. 2004. Can landscapes be read? In Palang, H. Sooväli, H., Antrop, M. & Setten, G. (eds.) *European rural landscapes: persistence and change in a globalising environment*, Dordrecht: Springer, 455-465.

Widgren, M. 2015. Linking Nordic landscape geography and political ecology. *Norsk Geografisk Tidsskrift-Norwegian Journal of Geography*, 69(4), 197-206.

Published book in the CLUES series

CLUES is an international scientific series covering PhD studies, scientific reports of contract research, conference proceedings, etc., in the fields of culture, history and heritage which have been written by, or were performed under the supervision of members of the research institute CLUE+

1. Door de lens van de landschapsbiografie (2015)
Een nieuwe kijk op de geschiedenis en het erfgoed van landschappen
Edited by Jan Kolen, Hanneke Ronnes & Rita Hermans
Paperback ISBN: 978-90-8890-313-7

2. Interdisciplinarity between Humanities and Science (2017)
A Festschrift in honour of Prof. Dr. Henk Kars
Edited by Sjoerd Kluiving, Lisette Kootker & Rita Hermans
Paperback ISBN: 978-90-8890-403-5

3. Treasures in Trusted Hands (2017)
Negotiating the Future of Colonial Cultural Objects
Jos van Beurden
Paperback ISBN: 978-90-8890-439-4

4. Reframing Luchino Visconti (2018)
Film and Art
Ivo Blom
Paperback ISBN: 978-90-8890-548-3

5. Unhinging the National Framework (2020)
Perspectives on Transnational Life Writing
Edited by Babs Boter, Marleen Rensen & Giles Scott-Smith
Paperback ISBN: 978-90-8890-974-0

6. Environmental humanities: a rethinking of landscape archaeology? (2021)
Interdisciplinary academic research related to different perspectives of landscapes
Edited by Sjoerd Kluiving, Kerstin Liden, Christina Fredengren
Paperback ISBN: 978-94-6427-003-7